THE
SECOND VATICAN
COUNCIL

——◄◆►——

The Story Behind the Ecumenical

Council of Pope John XXIII

THE SECOND

The Story Behind the Ecumenical

Translated by Alastair Guinan

HAWTHORN BOOKS INC.

VATICAN COUNCIL

Council of Pope John XXIII

HENRI DANIEL-ROPS

Publishers

New York

FIRST EDITION
March, 1962

NIHIL OBSTAT
Daniel V. Flynn, J.C.D.
CENSOR LIBRORUM

IMPRIMATUR
✠Francis Cardinal Spellman
ARCHIBISHOP OF NEW YORK

The nihil obstat and the imprimatur are official declarations that a book or pamphlet is free of doctrinal or moral error. No implication is contained therein that those who have granted the nihil obstat and imprimatur agree with the contents, opinions or statements expressed. *February 13, 1962*

Contents

I FROM SAINT PAUL'S DAY TO THE DAY OF JOHN XXIII   11

1. THE ILLUMINATION OF SAINT PAUL'S-WITHOUT-THE-WALLS   11

2. SAINT MATTHEW, XVIII, 20   14

3. THE "COUNCIL" ATTENDED BY SAINT PAUL   18

4. FROM PROVENCIAL ASSEMBLIES TO ECUMENICAL COUNCILS   21

5. HAVE THERE BEEN TWENTY-ONE COUNCILS?   25

6. THE DOCTRINAL COUNCILS OF THE EAST   30

7. THE COUNCILS OF MEDIEVAL CHRISTENDOM   33

8. THE COUNCIL AND THE POPE IN CONFLICT?   39

9. THE SPECTACULAR COUNCIL: TRENT   45

10. VATICAN I: THE UNCOMPLETED
COUNCIL 49

11. IS THE COUNCIL WHOLLY
UNEXPECTED? 55

II WHAT IS AN ECUMENICAL COUNCIL? 61

1. "IT HAS SEEMED GOOD TO THE
HOLY SPIRIT" 61

2. "ECUMENICAL" 65

3. POPE AND COUNCIL 68

4. "BISHOPS COMPOSE THE COUNCIL" 72

5. WHAT OF THE LAITY? 78

6. FROM THE ANNOUNCEMENT OF THE
COUNCIL TO THE CONVOCATION OF
THE CONCILIAR FATHERS 81

7. THE COUNCIL GOES INTO SESSION 86

8. "CONSENSI et SUBSCRIPSI": "I HAVE
AGREED AND SIGNED" 90

9. THE ACTA OF THE COUNCIL 94

10. "MANIFESTING" OF THE CHURCH 97

III THE OUTLOOK FOR THE SECOND
VATICAN COUNCIL 103

1. TWO YEARS PASS: THE "VIGIL OF
PENTECOST" 103

2. VATICAN II 106

3. THE COMMITTEES AT WORK 110

4. "SURVIVALS" AND "FORECAST" 117

5. A CRISIS IN THE CHURCH OR A CRISIS IN THE WORLD? 122

6. DOCTRINAL PERSPECTIVES 129

7. PASTORAL PERSPECTIVES 134

8. MISSIONARY AND APOSTOLIC PERSPECTIVES 139

9. ECUMENICAL PERSPECTIVES 144

10. THE COUNCIL OF JOHN XXIII 152

TRANSLATOR'S NOTE 157

THE AUTHOR AND HIS BOOK 159

THE
SECOND VATICAN
COUNCIL

———————◄◆►———————

The Story Behind the Ecumenical

Council of Pope John XXIII

I

From Saint Paul's Day
to the Day of John XXIII

————————

1. THE ILLUMINATION OF SAINT PAUL'S-
WITHOUT-THE-WALLS

On JANUARY 25, 1959, His Holiness John XXIII went to the Basilica of Saint Paul's-Without-the-Walls on the road to Ostia in order to commemorate the conversion of the Apostle to the Gentiles. The Chair of Unity Octave was then closing. This is a time set apart for prayer and meditation to the end that the followers of Christ who have varying ecclesiastical affiliations might think upon his petition "that all may be one" and beg Him to lead all of His flock into one fold. At the end of the day's function, the Pope and the eighteen assisting cardinals withdrew into a hall adjoining the modern nave of the old monastic church. Here, in intimacy with his brethren, the Pope spoke. He spoke in his characteristic manner, compounded of naturalness and majesty, wherein his authority is graced by his simplicity and ease. The cardinals, as they came out, were unable to conceal the emotions which his words had aroused in them.

In the three months which had elapsed since he had been

raised to the Chair of Peter, the resourceful plans of Pope John, as the Romans had quickly recognized, were no longer to be taken as surprising. In small things or in large, all that he had to say had proved to be meaningful and to indicate his over-all intentions. It was recognized that a new climate stirred in the Vatican, and it seemed that this old man, in whom some observers had thought to see a pontiff for but a brief, stop-gap, period, was showing a youthfulness in his approach to problems and an unlooked for degree of initiative. Yet, scarcely anyone expected the decisions which John XXIII communicated to the cardinals on the morning of that January twenty-fifth.

On the afternoon of the same day, as though to curb the voice of rumor which, more or less correctly, began to be heard in the Eternal City, the press office of the Vatican issued a communiqué of about fifty words. The Pope, it was announced, had shared with his hearers some thoughts which had been stirring within him during these first three months of his reign. As Bishop of Rome, he confessed his concern for the serious problems, raised by an ever-increasing population, which caused constantly renewed difficulties in the Church's task. As supreme shepherd of Christ's flock, he deeply felt the menacing dangers which threatened the spiritual life of Christians, "those aberrations which are everywhere to be encountered," and that excessively avid devotion to merely material progress which increasing technical perfection has more and more fostered among men. To combat these dangers the Pope announced three means which he purposed to adopt: a diocesan synod was to be convened without delay to study the needs of souls in the city of Rome; Canon Law, as codified in 1917, was to be brought up to date; and an ecumenical council was to be convoked. The declaration of this third project was amplified. According to the Pope's ideas, this assembly of the Universal Church was to have as its object not only the spiritual betterment of the Christian family, but would serve, as well, as "an invitation to all separated brethren to join in seeking that unity of belief for which so many souls in every part of the world long today."

Of the three decisions thus made public, it is surely the third that is most significant. It must be said, however, that it was the least foreseen. A well-informed observer, the present Bishop Veuillot of Angers, then an official in the chancery of the Vatican Department of State, has noted that it caused "surprise." This seems an understatement, if one may judge from the comments which enlivened Roman gossip in the following weeks. But it was soon understood that the Pope himself shared to some degree in the general astonishment. When enlarging in the course of various messages and allocutions upon this part of his plan, John XXIII did not scruple to acknowledge it as being due to a clear motion of the Holy Spirit or, in any case, a special grace or insight granted to him. He declared: "Suddenly and unexpectedly we were struck, as it were, by thought of this, within the lowliness of our spirit." He said again, in his characteristic fashion, that "it sprang or had sprung up within us as does the first flower of an early springtime." And he added that it was this certainty of having been enlightened from on high which aroused in him what he himself termed "humble resolve to put it into action." *

We ought not be amazed at the astonishment which came over many clerics and laymen alike. Even some of the cardinals, we may be sure, were taken aback. Ever since October 20, 1870, after the entry of the Piedmontese soldiery into Rome through the Porta Pia, when Pope Pius IX had declared that the Vatican Council must be regarded as "adjourned *sine die*," although not finally concluded, it had appeared that the notion of an ecumenical council would not again bulk large

---

* In an article in *Unitas* (December 1959; January 1960) Père Daniel Stiernon places this "enlightenment" as dating from January 19, 1959.

in the thinking of Catholics in general. Hard upon the heels of that very declaration, one of the most persistent opponents of the new dogma of Papal Infallibility, Dr. Dollinger, the Munich theologian, had said that in "the new Church" which it had wrought there would be no place for a general Council. And, as a matter of fact, had not the Popes, since that date, shown that they considered it unnecessary to summon to Rome the representatives of world Christianity before deciding even major questions? If the opinions of the bishops were desired, it would henceforth be enough to write to them, as Pius XII had actually done before, in the full exercise of his pontifical jurisdiction, when he proclaimed the dogma of Our Lady's Assumption.

But, even as the newspapers of the whole world saw in the announcement of the projected ecumenical council an historic event of far-reaching significance, the man who had resolved upon this project went forward with plans that gave testimony to his "humble resolution to put the plan into action." Certainly, no doubt arose that this was a decision of providential needfulness. As a theologian and an historian, how could he have failed to recognize that, by fixing upon this plan, he had set himself squarely in the very core of ecclesiastical tradition by responding to the exigencies of his own day in accordance with the age-long experience of the Church?

2. SAINT MATTHEW, XVIII, 20

As an institution, a council is not an element embodied in the basic constitution of the Church. Its existence is not necessary to Catholicity as is, for example, faith in the seven sacraments or in the primacy of Peter. Even if, down through the centuries, no council had ever met, the Catholic Church, Apostolic and Roman, directed by its visible head, the Vicar of Christ, would not have ceased to be. But it would certainly be wearing a different aspect than that which we now behold.

Strictly speaking, Jesus Christ is not the founder of the conciliar system. For this reason, councils are not said to stem directly from divine law but to depend upon the Church's legislative authority or canonical power. Actually, it was the Church which, acting spontaneously, gave birth to the institution we call the council. In so doing, however, the Church based this action on a profound sense of the Master's teaching. Moreover, the role of these reunions of Christendom occurring over a period of nineteen hundred years in the formation of Christianity has been of such a nature that it is difficult for a believer to shut his eyes here to that working of God's finger to which Bossuet has paid such high tribute.

As is true of most of what Christianity has established, the roots of this institution are in the Bible, and can be traced to prototypes in the fruitful ground of old Israel. The notion that the leader who seeks to fulfill the will of God is to do so in collaboration with the community of all believers is encountered very frequently in explicit or implied form in the Old Testament. Moses, although invested by Yahweh with power which appears boundless, was nevertheless ordered by Him to associate with himself a council of seventy wise men and even, on occasion, to have recourse to the assemblage of the people. No matter how powerful the kings of Israel were, it was incumbent upon them to take council with the whole nation as represented by the heads of the leading families and the priests. After the return of Israel from the Babylonian captivity, this consultation seems to have become almost fixed in an obligatory sense. In *Esdras* and *Nehemiah*, mention is often made of a "full assembly"—sometimes interpreted as a "full congregation"—brought together for the purpose of settling difficult problems, as, for example, in chapter five of *Nehemiah*, where the social problem is in question. At the time Jesus came to give His own testimony, everything tends to indicate that Judaic life was a community affair in which the people, as well as the chieftains, played a role and exercised a responsibility, mainly through the action of their various representatives, the most notable of whom were to be found in the Sanhedrin.

That Jesus conformed to His own national tradition is only what we should expect. In order that He might bring into being that new Israel which His Church was to be, He did not rest content with establishing only the College of Twelve— those apostolic pillars of the Church. He associated with them the seventy-two disciples, selected from the body of His followers at large, making of them auxiliary apostles, likewise involved in the task of preaching the Gospel. His whole course of conduct manifests the kind of feeling He had for the spiritual needs and the natural tendencies of the people with whom He was dealing. According to the vision of things which He unveiled, salvation is no merely individualistic thing. A man is not saved in isolation from his fellows; each must pray for the brethren; each must bear the other's burdens.* It is within the core of the brotherhood that salvation is wrought. How magnificently is this expressed in a Gospel verse, one of Matthew's most beautiful renderings of the Master's thought. "Whenever two or three are gathered together in My name, there am I, in the midst of them."

This note is even further emphasized. On Pentecost, when there was enacted that mysterious beginning of the work of the Church in which the Holy Spirit, whose coming Christ had foretold, descended upon the first Christians, who were they who received His enlightening flames? The Apostles, the Virgin Mother of Our Lord, and the seventy-two, alike. Indeed, the number recorded by *Acts* indicates that we are here

---

* Cf. the New Testament statement of this, which has bulked so large in the Christian monastic liturgical life: "*Alter alterius onera portate: et sic adimplebitis legem Christi.*" [Translator's note.]

confronted with an enlarged fraternity; for it speaks of one hundred and twenty of the brethren. Why had they come together? Was it merely to pray, to share past recollections, to prepare for the future? Yet all heard the great wind which marked the Spirit's coming. Those tongues of fire descended upon all. All were thenceforth made witnesses to Christ, all heralds of His Word; for to all was given the mysterious gift of tongues. One hundred twenty souls, then, constituted the representative body of the few hundred who made up the Church. This is of prime importance; and if it be not enough to demonstrate, as Gregory Magnus seems to have thought, "the divine origin of the conciliar system," it, at least, is sufficient to show that at the very commencement of the apostolic age, at the very time when the Church prepared to go forth from the Cenacle in order to undertake the conquest of the world, there was grouped around the leaders whom Christ had given to the Church a body politic, an assembly which could lawfully claim to be led by the Spirit.

It is likewise true that *Acts,* that moving account of the birth-pangs of Christianity, also indicates that the Church comprised an hierarchical organization of settled nature, based upon the undisputed primacy of Peter, a government by the College of the Apostles, and a means of taking counsel in necessary instances with all the faithful. Not only is the Apostolic College a real corporation in which the Twelve set forth their ideas, but the whole body of the Church shows itself to be a community in which the lowliest of the faithful are drawn to share in the making of decisions which touch them. As an example, we recognize that the deacons who were charged with the "duties of the table" (that is to say, with administrative detail) were chosen by the assembly. This is the assembly of which it is written that it had but one mind and one heart— *cor unum et anima una.* In any matter of a serious nature, the head of the body, the prince of the Apostles, did not wish to act solely upon his own initiative; rather he called upon the representatives of the community. It was in consort with them that he rendered his decision. The principle is thus established upon which we may rightly ground the conciliar system. One example will demonstrate how it functioned at the very beginning of the Church's life.

3. THE "COUNCIL" ATTENDED BY SAINT PAUL

WE ARE NOW concerned with the year 49 or 50, about two decades after the death of Jesus. The Church has enlarged, and it now definitely numbers thousands in its ranks, having gained many among those Jews who have accepted the Crucified as their Messiah; but it also encompasses adherents who have come from among the pagans, chiefly, of course, from those sympathizers with Jewish monotheism who are termed the "god fearing." This great influx of alien elements into a predominantly Judaic body has raised a delicate problem. Although the Gospel of Jesus transcended and went infinitely beyond the older revelation, it was not couched in terms requiring a break with it. "I am come to fulfill the Law, not to destroy it" are the words of the Master Himself. On the basis of this declaration and of similar statements some Christians of Jewish origin thought that if anyone were to enter the Christian Church, he must, first of all, submit himself to the requirements of the Mosaic Law. On the other hand, there were also some Christians who felt this to be beside the point. Speedily, therefore, there arose tension between the two groups—the *Judaisers* and the *Hellenists*.

That such a man as Peter put himself into the opposition on the matters of relations with the pagans indicates how delicate the question had become. When, after having preached the Gospel on the shore of the Mediterranean, he learned that a pagan, the Centurion of Cesarea, wished to be admitted into the Church, he was much disturbed. In a state of ecstasy on a roof-top in Joppa, where he had prayed for divine enlightenment, he saw all possible kinds of nourishment being set out for him by Heaven. At first, he refused to partake, protesting that he was not accustomed to eat unless he knew that the flesh of the animals before him had been properly slaughtered, and the fruits of the earth to have been legally tithed. When he awoke, he understood that this vision was from Heaven and that its object was to redeem him from mere strictness of observance. Thus did he come to realise that he might receive as a brother a pagan of good will like Cornelius, even though he had been nourished upon food technically termed impure.

The whole question presented itself most pressingly in pagan surroundings, beyond Palestine, to which, ever more and more, the Good News was being brought. The greater the number of pagans who came into the Church, the less necessary did it appear that they pass through the half way house of Judaism before accepting the new belief. Moreover, of all the practices which the Torah required, the custom enjoining circumcision aroused among the pagans an insurmountable degree of distaste. Was it really necessary to require circumcision of converts at the risk of having countless numbers of them refuse Christian baptism rather than submit to this rite? At Rome, where salacious jokes about the "skinned" were part of the stock of comic plays, it seemed certain that to require enforcement of the Jewish custom would mean abandonment of the apostolate.

The man who, first and most firmly, set his face against the enforcement of this custom was that convert from Judaism, that old student of the rabbis of the Pharisees whom Christ, by touching his heart with His own finger, had Himself won to His cause. Ever since the time on the road to Damascus when

Saul of Tarsus had been thrown to earth by blinding light and had heard himself called by name, every fibre of his being had been bent to one purpose, that he might extend the triumphant reign of the Church he had hitherto persecuted. His nature, as well as the influences which had made and formed him and had opened his mind to broader understanding, had led him to conclude that the problem of Judaic observances was a most serious matter which would have to be handled correctly unless the rise of Christianity were to be impeded. Had he not, himself, moreover clashed, in violent opposition with the Judaisers? Wherever he had preached, even in pagan towns far removed from Palestine, he found some members of the local Jewish society—those of that *Diaspora* from Israel who were everywhere to be encountered—who would say to his catechumens: "You can never be saved unless you will accept circumcision." *Acts* tells us that the discussions on this subject became the occasion of altercations and brawlings.

Paul had therefore arrived at a meaningful decision. He was now resolved to go to Jerusalem and to lay before the authorities these difficulties with his own request that they be decisively settled. In the company of his faithful Barnabas and some of the brethren, he came to the holy city, where there was then held a reunion of major significance. The fifteenth chapter of *Acts* affords us the minutes of this meeting. Not only the Apostles were present, but also, as the text tell us, the *presbyters*. This term is derived from a Greek word, and from it our own word for *priests* comes: it means an older man. Among the Jews it had also the connotation of notable or "senator;" and it was used especially in referring to members of the Sanhedrin. Some modern translations of the Gospel render it as elder or ancient. As the primitive Church is pictured for us by *Acts* and the *Epistles,* we see so designated the rectors of churches and the leading spirits in the direction of local groups of believers; and the word becomes analogous to the title of bishop. This meeting at Jerusalem of which I am now speaking—this "first council," as it is often called, with what is, perhaps, some exaggeration—this meeting joined together not only the Apostolic leaders of the Church but also the bishops (or elders) who represented the Church as a whole. There is much significance here.

The decision in respect to the question which had been made the occasion of this council is well known. We are aware of how, after the forceful intervention of James, that holy man whose fidelity in matters Judaic was beyond question, the open conception of the nature of Christianity prevailed over narrower views. Peter, James, and John joined hands with Paul and Barnabas in brotherhood, and a written decree was put forth expressing what was, henceforward, to be the rule throughout Christendom. Converts were not to be bound by any other burden than these essential ones: that they abstain from partaking of food which has been offered to idols by having been burnt in honor of them, and from fornication. The council, a meeting of the bishops, had established a doctrinal norm, and had endowed the Church with a definite point of view. It was to this double task that, down through the centuries, the many similar meetings which followed this one were to devote themselves.

4. FROM PROVINCIAL ASSEMBLIES TO ECUMENICAL COUNCILS

YET, WE SHALL have to wait a long time—for almost three centuries—before the birth of what can be called an ecumenical council. It is not true that, in the interval, Christians had lost the taste for assembling their leaders that they might render decisions. The contrary is true; for, in the same proportion that Christianity spread itself throughout the empire, so did the inclination increase to fashion its administrative functioning upon that of imperial Rome. As one illustration, I may note that it was the accepted geographical lines of imperial determination which set the pattern for the diocese of the Church. Christian assemblies continued to follow the model established by the city meeting of Greece and of Rome; and some Catholic historians, as for instance Bishop Batiffol, have even thought that these assemblies adopted procedural methods of the provincial assemblies of the empire and even those of the Roman Senate itself. Nevertheless, the Church, then a persecuted sect, was obliged to live, more or less, as if under a cloud; it would have been fatal to attempt a meeting of all its parts. Accordingly, only within a province or, at most, within a region, were such assemblies held prior to the fourth century.

The history of these provincial councils is far from well-known. The records of many have perished; there are many of which no ecclesiastical historian has treated. Some were certainly held in all parts of the Church—in the East as well as in Africa; in Italy, as well as in Gaul and in Spain. Why was this done? It seems, ordinarily, that it was for the purpose of settling administrative matters and in order to establish a line of conduct; less frequently to enact a law, but most often to set up means by which doctrinal deviation might be countered. Thus, when the fanatical Montanus began to propagate his apocalyptic notions in Asia Minor during the second century, a provincial council was convened against him in Phrygia. Eusebius tells us of this; as he does also of another which was convoked in response to an appeal from Pope Victor with the intent of finding an end to the controversies over the date of Easter which were upsetting the Church. In 220, Agrippinus, Bishop of Carthage, initiated a series of provincial councils in Africa; in 256, his successor, St. Cyprian, called together a council of eighty-seven bishops that they might pronounce the invalidity of baptisms conferred by heretics. We know, too, that councils were held at Elvira in Spain and likewise in the Orient, at Antioch and Iconkum, and at Alexandria in Egypt. And in 314, a short while before the first council termed in history an ecumenical council—that of Nicea— thirty-three representatives of Western Christianity assembled at Arles to take measures against the heretical schism of the intransigent Donatus.

So it was that, during the first three centuries, Church assemblies gradually assumed an institutional character. In the West, we find Tertullian calling such meetings *councils,* while, in the East, the term *synod,* favoured by Dionysius of Alexandria, was in use. These two words, one Latin, the other Greek, evoked both the idea of meeting and that of place. At first, these assemblies were composed not of bishops alone but also of priests and deacons, and even laymen were included, at least as observers. But, in the third century, it was established that only the bishops made the decisions; other clerics were there only as consultors. In its provincial form—a form which was destined to last a long time, indeed, in a sense, to our own day —the conciliar institution perfected itself as an instrument by which, after the triumph of the Church in the Empire, it became possible to bring together all the representatives of Christianity. Thus begins a new stage in the development of Church government.

The enlargement of this institution to the world-wide importance which it thus gained was one of the achievements— and he ought be given credit for this—of Emperor Constantine. When he had won at the Milvean Bridge his victory over his rival, Maxentius, in a manner which tradition marks as miraculous (recall the celebrated phrase, *In hoc Signo vinces;* In this Sign thou shall conquer) the new master of imperial Rome showed himself master, as well, of the Roman Church, which he really aided, and to which his edict, promulgated at Milan, gave freedom. Yet the solicitude which he displayed for the Church was such that, though it appeared touching to some, struck many as less desirable. Even while still un-baptized—for he waited for twenty-five years to accept the laver of regeneration—he plunged fully into every religious question of his age. Most delicate of all these was that aroused by the trouble which the rapid development of Arian heresy had caused. To Arius, a priest of Alexandria, it had seemed that Christ was not God, equal to the Father, but rather a creature—perfect, the first-born of creation, yet not embody-ing the divine essence. These ideas set the whole of Eastern Christendom on fire. A provincial council held at Alexandria had served only to add fuel to the conflagration for, in sen-tencing the heretic and expelling him from Egypt, it served only to spur him on to find another ground for his dangerous teaching. The emperor, while freely confessing these theolog-ical fine points to be beyond him, was aware that in spite of all his power he could not stem this tide unless aided by a more spiritual force than his own. He therefore decided to call to-gether qualified representatives from every city of the Em-pire, throughout the *world*, in Greek, *oikoumene*. The spot chosen for this meeting was Nicea in Bythinia, close by the sea of Marmora and the city of Byzantium. Here then, on May 20, 325, in an atmosphere of high fervor, the opening session of the first ecumenical council was held.

Actually, this first ecumenical council was not fully rep-resentative of the whole church. Of the three hundred and twenty-eight bishops present—some say, two hundred and fifty—there were but few from the West, despite the en-thusiastic assurance of Eusebius who tells us that "the chief of God's ministers had come from every part of Europe." The large majority was made up of men from Syria, Cilicia, Pales-tine, Egypt, Macedonia, Thrace, Libya, and Mesopotamia; but the bishops from the West could be counted on the fingers of one hand. Outstanding among them was Hosius of Cordova, noted as a vigorous adversary of the Egyptian heretic. But this fact is of lesser importance than the assertion of the principle of universality. Until that time, the competence of provincial councils and synods had been but ill-defined: whatever they might claim to be by tradition, their actual authority stemmed from the acceptance which the Church would give to the decisions they took. Henceforth, by reason alone of the claim that it represented the whole church in principle, the ecumenical council would be able to set itself up as a final authority.

It must be added that at Nicea another determining principle was acknowledged, a principle which in the course of time was to become all-conclusive, namely that with the council was joined the Bishop of Rome, the Pope. The Pope at that time was Saint Sylvester who, because his advanced years made the long journey into Asia impossible, sent in his stead two of his priests, Vitus and Vicentius, to whom he expressly delegated his own powers.

Thus do we see a new step in conciliar development. The institution now exhibits three definite characteristics: it is an assembly of bishops, it is universal in principle, and the Pope is part of it. Confirmed by time and strengthened in their application, these characteristics are to become the criteria by which the definition of an ecumenical council is expressed, even if these criteria do not guarantee that we can draw up a wholly undisputed list of councils.

5. HAVE THERE BEEN TWENTY-ONE COUNCILS?

ASTONISHING AS the fact may seem, there does not exist an official list of the councils which the Catholic Church recognises as ecumenical. Juridically, they are quite distinct from other meetings which are called by the name of council—from provincial councils at which the local metropolitan archbishop presides, or plenary councils held under the presidency of a pontifical legate, which can be of major importance in the life of the Church, as were the three held during the last century at Baltimore. These made American Catholicism what it now is. Ecumenical councils are even more sharply to be distinguished from those administrative meetings, provincial synods and meetings of the bishops, held on a national level, like those at which the cardinals and archbishops of France assemble twice yearly; like the occasional meetings of the French ordinaries, like such international meetings as was the Conference of Manila for the Far East in 1958 or that in South America in 1960.

Yet it is not always easy to exercise this necessary discrimination. How is the ecumenical nature of a council to be defined? Is it by the willingness of those who are met to join with representatives of the whole church? It is not certainly established that such willingness existed at all times before the year 1000. Is it by the acceptance of the councils' decisions in some official act of the universal Church, as in fact occurs in pontifical sanction? As far as a number of the councils is concerned their ecumenicity is established only by the way in which the Church subsequently acted.

Even in respect to some relatively recent councils, the historical framework into which certain of them must be set allows us to call into question not only their ecumenical character but their very existence. The Council of Florence, held from 1438 1439, is an example. Despite its great interest as having effected a momentary reconciliation between the Eastern Orthodox Church and the Roman Church, should we consider it a distinct council, or is it not rather a continuation of that which opened at Bâle in 1431? And is this Council of Bâle, called into being by a Pope, but rebelling against him, to

be considered a true council? In 1409-1410 there was held at Pisa, during the dire days of the Great Western Schism, a council in which some three hundred well-meaning prelates thought to end that catastrophe. They succeeded only in adding to the confusion by electing a third Pope. Is this council rightfully called ecumenical? Such an admission would bring the figures up to twenty-two councils. Certain historians have maintained this to be so, but they could not do so today. For, by taking the name John XXIII, the present Sovereign Pontiff has nullified the election of his namesake, reducing the Pope of Pisa, who succeeded Alexander V under the same title, to the status of an "anti-Pope." Thus the present occupant of Peter's Chair has rejected the authority of the Pisan Council. But even in the more traditionally favored list, that which numbers the councils at twenty-one, there are some councils whose authenticity has been under dispute. One is the Fourth Council of Constantinople, convoked by Emperor Basil I (the Macedonian) in 869 to subdue the Patriarch Photius. This council is rejected by the Eastern Orthodox Church which held a synod that rehabilitated the condemned man. In the view of that learned canonist and historian, Cardinal Jacobozzo, of the five councils held at the Lateran between 1123 and 1512, the first two are deemed unacceptable, as is also that of Bâle.*
According to the French and Spanish prelates who sat at Trent, all five of the Lateran councils were unacceptable. When everything is taken into consideration, it is likely that the Second Vatican Council will bear the number twenty-second; but this will not be a result of historical demonstration.

---

* Bâle is considered to be a "false council" for four reasons: 1. because the council was excommunicated by Eugenius IV; 2. because it set up an anti-Pope who subsequently acknowledged his fault and made his submission; 3. because not one of its decrees was ever given papal approval; 4. because its decree on the Immaculate Conception of Our Lady is so widely considered nugatory and unacknowledged that the definition of the doctrine by Pius IX on December 8, 1854, is regarded as a new statement of that ancient belief.

TABLE OF THE COUNCILS

No.	Date	Pope	Place of Meeting	Principal Achievements
1	325	Sylvester I	Nicea	The Creed against Arianism
2	381	Damasus I	Constantinople I	Confirmation and explanation of the Nicene Creed
3	431	Celestine I	Ephesus	Mary as *the Mother of God* vindicated against Nestorianism
4	451	Leo I Magnus	Chalcedon	Definition of the two natures of Christ
5	553	Vigilius	Constantinople II	Fuller condemnation of Nestorianism
6	680-681	Agatho and later Leo II	Constantinople III	Condemnation of Monothelism (the doctrine of but one will in Christ)
7	787	Adrian I	Nicea II	Authorisation of the use of images
8	869-870	Nicholas I Adrian II	Constantinople IV	Against Photius
9	1123	Calixtus II	Lateran I	Termination of the Investiture Dispute
10	1139	Innocent II	Lateran II	End put to the schism of Anacletus
11	1179	Alexander III	Lateran III	Opposition to Frederick Barbarosa; Establishment of rules for Papal elections
12	1215	Innocent III	Lateran IV	Condemnation of the Cathari; Decree of annual Confession and Holy Communion; Definition of Transubstantiation
13	1245	Innocent IV	Lyon I	Deposition of Frederick II
14	1274	Gregory X	Lyon II	Reunion with the Greeks; Regulation of the Conclave
15	1312	Clement V	Vienne in Dauphine, France	Decree of reform following on the condemnation of the Templars
16	1414-1418	Ended by Martin V	Constance	End of the Great Schism; Condemnation of John Hus
?	1437	Convoked by Eugenius IV	Bale (Disputed)	The Council in opposition to the Pope
17	1437-1439	Eugenius IV	Ferrara-Florence	Union with the Greeks
18	1512-1517	Julius II	Lateran V	Opposition to Conciliar plans of Louis XII; Decrees of reform
19	1543-1563	From Paul III to Pius IV	Trent	Defense against Protestantism; General Reform of the Church
20	1869-1870	Pius IX	Vatican I	Primacy and Infallibility of the Pope

Four great divisions may be noted in the list of councils. The first is that of the period of the Golden Age which marks the day anterior to the break between East and West, and during which eight councils offered to the world the picture of the ecclesiastical communion of all Christendom in the fullness of its universal and apostolic authority. The second state is that of the seven councils following. These are sometimes called the "Christian Councils," because they take their place within the framework of that regime which marks the medieval West as being Christendom. It was at this time that the papal supremacy was so successfully affirmed. Following this comes a period of stress and agitation: the council rises up against the papal supremacy, and we face a crisis which tore the Church asunder, despite the fact that, during those trying days, an effort at reuniting East and West was momentarily successful. In the fourth stage, two great councils fill the period, The Council of Trent and the First Vatican Council by which the modern Church, the Church as we know it, was built up in its doctrinal and institutional aspects.

It is noteworthy that not one of these gatherings, even those of which the authenticity of their authority is in dispute, has been without usefulness or significance. It might be said that "the history of the councils is, in some sense, the history of the Church's life as she has faced the growth of successive crises in her confrontation with the changing worlds, with the evolution of human thought, and with successive cultural influences." * Different causes have been at the root of the varied nature of the different councils: certain of them have regarded as their essential task the settlement of some doctrinal question; some have responded to the Church's need for reorganization, even for reformation and for purification; others, and this is notably true of Trent, have shown themselves to be fertile in plans for dogmatic, organizational, and disciplinary reconstruction.

"The new strength to fulfill her divine mission," which John XXIII has stated he expects the Church to draw from the Second Vatican Council, is really just what history tells us marks these great gatherings; and from them the Church has been given fruitful inspiration in every age. Each council displays in its own way, but still in the fullest sense, a will to accommodate to the needs of the day—as both Pius IX and

---

* Bishop Veuillot.

John XXIII have said—those everlasting truths which the councils exist to serve, and which are, more or less, masked and concealed from men by misunderstanding or tedium. The task of the councils is to lead men to the vision of the light they require to cope with the duties and the needs of their own time.

6. THE DOCTRINAL COUNCILS OF THE EAST

THE FIRST eight ecumenical councils recognised by the Catholic Church have in common something which to men of our time is surprising. All were held in the East, and—if we except the last of them—the Eastern Orthodox Church recognises their decisions as valid. They antedated the sad events which, by reason of obstinacy and mistakes of which both sides were guilty, led to the break in relations in 1054 between Michael Cerularius, the Patriarch of Constantinople, and Pope Leo IX. It is true that the circumstances under which these eight councils met and sat are unlike those which we should wish to see today surrounding an ecclesiastical assemblage. Following the lead of Constantine, it was the emperor, the *basileus*, of Constantinople, whoever he might be, who customarily took it upon himself to call upon the bishops to join together for the purpose of considering deep spiritual questions, even though those rulers might sometimes have blood-stained hands or be men whose personal religious convictions were uncertain, as was the case of Constantine himself. It even came about that two empresses, the energetic Pulcheria and the artful Irene, prone to be theologians, set themselves up as patrons of the council and were quick to interfere in conciliar deliberations, sometimes indiscreetly but never unintelligently. Not one of these assemblies ever degenerated into that downright rivalry between the rabble and the authorities that marked the regional council of 449, which has become celebrated in history as the Robber-Council of Ephesus. But there was no one of them in which secular political forces failed to exert an influence not always favourable to the Church's interest. If it be recalled that the Pope was not always represented, it will seem that one might be tempted to look with misgiving at certain of these Eastern councils.

Nevertheless, they have played a major role in the history of dogma. With the single exception of the last, the Fourth Council of Constantinople, which met in 869-70 under the great dome of Hagia Sophia in order to determine the case of Photius, each was essentially occupied with doctrinal matters. This is not to say that other questions were not studied: examples to the contrary lie in the consideration of the date of Easter, or of the matter of priestly training, or of the requirements for the consecration of bishops. And it is curious to note that almost everyone considered the money question in order to condemn usury. But, if one seeks the essential note of the accomplishments of these seven councils, one must look to the plane of fundamental theological matters.

Yet, even in this domain, it may be quite disconcerting to dwell upon some particulars. How unimportant are those interminable discussions about what seems no more than trifling details, like the famous iota which distinguishes *homoous-ios* from *homoiousios?* Is it not to indulge in over-refined hairsplitting to ask whether Christ be consubstantially like unto, or of identical substance with, the Father? All that the use of the adjective "Byzantine" can mean by way of depreciation to a modern mind trained according to Cartesian principles and prone to simplify matters is perfectly illustrated by the great debates which took place at every one of these meetings. Nevertheless, it would be to misjudge the history of Christianity and its beliefs were one to persist in this hasty judgement.

It is characteristic of oriental Christians, who have been brought up on the wine of Greek philosophical thought, to peer deeply into the basic metaphysical problems, those of the Trinity, the divinity of the Word, that of the Holy Spirit, the world's coming into being, and the problem of evil. In the Occident, on the other hands, theological speculation has been rather subjective, having been brought chiefly to bear upon man and his freedom of will, on grace, predestination, faith and good works, and on the ethical life. It was their passion for metaphysics which lay at the root of all that welter of heretical thought which marks the history of oriental Christians and which has, moreover, condemned many Western minds to dumb wonderment in the face of it. How can one distinguish among all those Arians, Semi-Arians, Anómeans, Homóeans, all those Patripassionists and Subordinationists, all those Macedonians who came not indeed from Macedonia but were followers of a certain Patriarch, Macedonius, (and who are, moreover, known also as Pneumotomachians?) However, as His Holiness John XXIII remarked in his allocution of November 14, 1960, it is because of these heresies and errors that, in some sense, by way of argumentation against them, some of the most important dogmatic truths have been declared after the most careful scrutiny of divergent formulations of them.

During those first five centuries in which the first seven of the ecumenical councils were held—to say nothing of the great number of provincial councils, diocesan synods, assemblies of bishops wherein discussion proceeded almost uninterruptedly—an attempt was made to plumb and to illumine the truths contained in Scripture, and to express them in succinct form. To this effort the Church owes much.

Thus it is to the First Nicene Council, whose work was confirmed and extended five years later by the First Council of Constantinople, that the Church is indebted for the definition of God as being One and Triune, a single essence in three Persons, a concept in which every Christian professes his belief when, at High Mass there is intoned the *Nicene Creed*. It is because of the Chalcedon Council, the largest of those of the first thousand years, held in 451, in concord with Saint Leo Magnus and in the presence of his legates that all believers profess the dogmatic truth that in Christ there are two natures, distinct and untransformed, undivided and united. Likewise it is because Saint Cyril, the great Bishop of Alexandria, was able to effect, amid stormy conciliar sessions at Ephesus in 431, the acceptance of his thesis in opposition to Nestorian ideas, that we have the right to call the Virgin Mary the Mother of God —*Theotokos*—thus subscribing to a formulary which many Catholics would think can never even have been called into question.

Therefore these Eastern councils must be granted a place whose importance in Church history cannot be overestimated. Had they not been held, had theologians not engaged in rough contests at them, there are many essential points of dogmatic belief which would have remained long unfixed.

7. THE COUNCILS OF MEDIEVAL CHRISTENDOM

Two HUNDRED and twenty-six years passed without any council sitting, and when a new meeting did convene it was not in the Orient. Nor did it bear much resemblance to those that had gone before; for, with the passage of time, the world had changed. As Byzantium sank from glory, there arose in the West a new power. Out of the chaos of barbarism, amid bloodshed and tribulation, the Church slowly fostered a new culture. In order to do this, it made itself all things to all men, becoming a part of every kind of human activity, civic, political, economic, and intellectual. In a literal sense the Church and society were one. For a period of three hundred years, the West was to live under this regime in which religion impregnated secular affairs and in which the temporal encroached upon the ecclesiastical. This was the age of Western Christendom.

At this same time, Western Christianity became subject to influences which bound it more strictly to the Roman See by means of a strict hierarchical system of which the Vicar of Christ was the head. The Pope, chief shepherd of the Church, was likewise the guide and the pilot of Christianity.

The council yielded to these changed influences. No longer was it a field for the discussion of only great religious questions; it became an arena for the manifestation of the interests of Christian society as a whole. As Church assemblies, the councils of this stage of the institution's development seemed to gather together all Christendom. In the history of the Church these councils were to play a great part, and in profane history their role cannot be overlooked. Between 1123 and 1312 we are able to count seven of them.

Although the empire had been set up again in the West by help of the Church, the emperor no longer would exercise the initiative in convening councils. The plan formed by Charlemagne in 787, to assemble a Western council which would take the place of the council then sitting at Nice, was of short duration and was not imitated successfully. As for the Germanic emperor, Henry III, it was not his intention to assert the ecumenicity of the modest gathering which he caused to assemble at Sutri in 1047 for the purpose of resolving the problem raised by three candidates in rivalry for the papal crown. It was rather the Popes who, slowly and gradually as Christian institutions settled into place, were induced to summon to their side representatives of all Christendom to assist their direction of the Church.

The old custom of having diocesan and provincial synods had not died out. In countries like Spain it even yet counted for much. The Popes were accustomed to invite visiting bishops to attend sessions of the Roman Synods. As the scope of the meetings grew greater, they increased in importance. In 1059, when Nicholas II promulgated his celebrated decree reserving to the cardinals the right to elect the Pope, he had with him one hundred and thirteen bishops. When Gregory VII undertook those vast plans of reform with which his name will ever be linked, he was assisted by gatherings composed of international representatives. Somewhat later, at the Roman Council of 1116, there might have been counted four hundred and twenty-seven participants who had come from at least eight different countries. It was but natural, therefore, for these assemblies to take on an international character. But the word *ecumenical* had been so linked to another kind of meeting that it was not used in reference to them, and they were rather spoken of as general councils. It was only afterward, during the Tridentine period, that attention was given to the criteria of ecumenicity and that an attempt was made to spell them out. But notwithstanding this, the councils held after 1123 were indeed ecumenical.

The marks of these councils of Western Christendom are definite. From the beginning, they were convoked by the Pope or, in any case, under his mandate; a *dictatus papale* attributed —it must be said, erroneously—to Gregory VII, declares, "No synod may be considered as being general if it lacks the Pope's approval of it as such." The agenda for each day had to be prepared by the officials of the Roman Curia, and plenary sessions were held under the presidency of papal legates. All the nations of Christendom were called to these assemblies, their representatives being more or less numerous according to circumstances, the importance of the matters under consideration, and the strength and force of the reigning Pontiff. More than eight hundred attended the Fourth Lateran Council, convoked by Innocent III, then in his heyday; but there were scarcely one hundred and fifty at the First Council of Lyon, when it was a question of condemning the redoubtable Emperor Frederick II. These representatives of Christendom were not all bishops. Abbots of monastic foundations, delegates of the religious orders, and even laymen, princes, kings and emperors (who might attend either in person or by ambassadorial delegates) also were present. Inasmuch as the matters which came under discussion affected Christendom as a political and civic society, it was thought that laymen should attend in accordance with the old axiom of Roman public law which declares: "Everyone has a right to be heard in the discussion and approval of what concerns all men." And, actually, this congregation about the person of the Pontiff of so many powerful personages could not fail to reflect some glory upon him. Who could doubt this in seeing at the Fourth Lateran Council in 1215 the Latin Emperor of Constantinople, the Kings of Germany, of France, of England, of Jerusalem, of Aragon, of Portugal and of Hungary, represented by their greatest lords, and dozens of great nobles attending in their own person?

For what reason were the seven councils of Western Christendom convened? With the exception of one which can be regarded as being held for the secret purpose of stemming imperial rivalry by advertising papal power, all were occasioned by some crisis in the Church. In 1123, the First Lateran Council put an end to the investiture controversy; in 1139, the Second Lateran Council sought to compose the schism caused by the simultaneous elections of two popes, Innocent II and Anacletus; in 1179, the Third Lateran Council set itself up against the overweening ascendency of emperor Frederick Barbarossa. After the Fourth Lateran Council, at which Innocent III was at the apogee of his power, it was the ever increasing tension between papacy and empire which provoked the calling of three councils. The transfer of the locale of their setting into France serves to show that the papal supremacy was threatened from more than one quarter. At the First Council of Lyon in 1245, Emperor Frederick II was declared deprived of his powers in a dramatic ceremony. At the Second Council of Lyon, in 1245, Christendom attempted to launch an offensive expressive of the anxiety it felt at seeing its territories in the Holy Land collapsing under the blows of the Turks. The unhappy Council of Vienne, in Dauphine, was held in 1311-12 at a time when the affair of the Templars pointed out only too well how much danger from the ambitions of France's king and the anarchic conditions prevalent in Italy had been menacing the Holy See ever since the outrage at Agnani.

But it would be an error to believe that these seven councils were confined to debating the problems which had determined their convocation. If all treated of the major Christian concerns of the day, as, for example, the Crusades or the truce of God, if some were obliged to deal with purely political matters, such as the relations between enemy sovereigns, the part these councils played in the history of the Church is far from being restricted to such matters. It may be admitted that they lack something of the broad theological vision which had marked their Byzantine predecessors: they gave little attention, even by way of surface consideration—much less in basic treatment—to important dogmatic problems, although they did definitively fix some doctrinal points. Thus, in the Fourth Lateran Council, the definition of Eucharistic Transubstantiation which still prevails was asserted. And the part played by the councils in the Church's battle with error was no mean one; for no important deviation from the norm, no heresy, cropped up which was not considered in a council, and all this necessitated serious doctrinal work. Conciliar condemnations were fulminated against the Albigensian Cathari and the *Pauvres de Lyon* or Waldensians. In one sense, these condemnations were more crucial than those which the oriental councils had formerly pronounced; for the whole of Christendom took them to heart and put them into effect by undertaking to destroy non-conformism. In 1274, the Second Council of Lyon—to which the Emperor Michael of Constantinople, the King of Armenia and his chief bishop or *Catholicos*, and even the Great Khan of the Mongols were invited— made a study, distinguished by intelligence and good will, of the matter of Church unity. Had it not been for the obstinate recoil of the Greek episcopate, the Council's efforts to resolve the difficulties might have been successful.

But it was in respect to ecclesiastical organisation and in the regulation of practical affairs in church life that the councils held during the age of mediaeval Christianity are proved to be most lasting in their effects. Many preceptive enactments which originated during this period are still part of Christian obligation, as is, for example, the obligation that every Catholic must go to confession and approach the Communion table at least once a year. This was a solemn enactment of the Fourth Lateran Council in 1215. The regulations which, even today, govern the manner of conducting a papal election are based upon decisions arrived at by the mediaeval councils: such provisions include the majority of two thirds set by the Third Lateran Council; the complete isolation of the conclave, and the obligation resting upon its members that they must choose a Pope before being permitted to quit their temporary confinement—all were established at the Second Council of Lyon. Likewise is it true that the wise rule which prohibits anyone who is not thirty years old from being raised to the episcopal office or elected a monastic abbot, is due to a conciliar decision—in this case, one made by the Third Lateran Council. A decisive attitude toward missionary work was set forth for the Church at the Council of Vienne, and this was under the impulsion of that genial Spaniard, Ramón Lul.

The Church of our own day owes more than is ordinarily thought to these mediaeval assemblies, alien as they seem to our modern ecclesiastical life.

8. THE COUNCIL AND THE POPE IN CONFLICT?

BUT ON THE agenda of every one of the mediaeval councils we find another matter: the whole question of reform. By this there is to be understood a sense of the obligation resting always upon the Church that it oppose those tendencies to gravitate in the direction of the lowest common denominator which man's inclinations to the way of least resistance pit against the laws of God and to the elevated inspirations which He grants. This implies a heavy task for the well-disposed, something from which they can never find rest, a very rock of Sisyphus—a labor ever to be undertaken but never to be completed. The whole course of history during the Middle Ages is marked by a succession of revivals followed by retrogressions. The matter of reforming men and institutions was an ever-present object of every ecumenical council. Not one of them prorogued before enacting canons condemning those two major cancers in the moral life of the Church— simony and priestly concubinage. Yet, as must sadly be noted, the efficiency of the methods presented as means of correcting vice never quite met the zeal of the hopes which had aroused them. Can it be that current ecclesiastical authority then lacked the vigor needed to implement the noble aspirations which the Christian conscience had voiced through these conciliar assemblies? Such indeed seems to have been the underlying reason for the dramatic crisis which arose in the fifteenth

century when the conciliar system and the Papacy found
themselves in conflict, pitted one against the other.

Throughout the Middle Ages, a genuine alliance actually
united these two forces, and their work was really collabora-
tive. The sense in which the members of the council owed sub-
missiveness to the Popes did not inhibit the bishops from expressing true freedom of opinion and freedom of action, as
well. Servility to the Pope was no part of any council's intent
or showing. At Vienne, the condemnation of the Templars
had probably been pronounced by a tribunal of the Inquisition
prior to the very first session of the Council, so certain did it
appear that that assembly would never vote it itself. But
this kind of autonomy walked hand in hand with that instinct
of unity which so thoroughly informed mediaeval Christianity, and with the conviction that that instinct found its best
expression in the Pope as visible head of the Church. However,
by the end of the fourteenth century, this position had undergone some modification. On the one hand, the disruption of
united Christianity had set in; its unity began to split under the
impulsions exerted by the national sovereignties. On the other
hand, the papal office itself was enfeebled by the weak nature
of some of those who held it. Its holders, expelled for a time
from Rome by the anarchic spirit which then infested Italy,
were unable to re-establish themselves in full force until Gregory XI put an end to the Avignon exile in 1377. The papacy
was even less well equipped to enforce a true reform of the
whole Church by reorganizing its structure and by separating
itself from the temporal concerns which had so largely come
to determine its whole outlook and inclination. After the glori-
ous return, Gregory XI died in an agony of anxiety about
what the future portended. The election of his successor led
to the Great Western Schism, destined to endure for thirty-
nine years, and partisans of conciliar, as opposed to papal,

authority seemed to carry the day as their ideas became wide-spread.

They were not without forerunners. As early as the thirteenth century, at the very time when Innocent III had raised the papacy to a point of high glory, his old master, Huguccio of Bologna, had maintained that, if the Pope were in error, authority would devolve upon a general council to set the Church to rights. One hundred years later, even as the last general assembly of medieval Christendom was in session at Vienne, Durandus, Bishop of Mende, had published a treatise on general councils in which the synodal constitution of the primitive Church was held up as a model. In the first half of the fourteenth century, those theoretical revolutionaries, Marsiglio of Padua and William of Ockham, had gone even further. Democrats born out of due time and advocates of the sovereignty of the people, they shared a conception of the papal office which reduced it to merely "representative" status, in an almost parliamentary sense of that word. The Pope was, they thought, only a delegate of the Universal Church, and his authority depended upon the mandate he had received. Forty years later, it seemed that the Great Western Schism demonstrated the truth of the dictum of the Parisian, Pierre d'Ailly, and the conciliar thesis thus began making the progress of an epidemic. Henri de Langenstein thought that an ecumenical council had greater authority than the Pope, and Conrad de Gelnhausen asserted that the universal coming together of all the delegates of the Church must be part of the ordinary administration of the Church.

Can such contentions be borne out by actual fact? If the confusion of the schism were to be resolved, would it not be required that a council be called? A first attempt of this nature failed miserably: it was the Pisan Council, convoked by the cardinals themselves and resulting only in the setting up of three popes in place of two. But at Constance in 1414, affairs took a turn for the better. In compliance with the request of Emperor Sigismund, John XXIII, the antipope of Pisa called this council despite his own lack of enthusiasm; and it held uncounted, unending, and unbelievable sittings amid scenes of all but constant confusion for four years. This was a singular council in which bishops were no more than a small minority in the midst of representatives of chapters, monasteries, universities, corporations, and sovereignties. Yet it finally attained the desired end. One after the other two of the contending popes resigned themselves to withdrawing from the field, and the third, the Pope of Avignon, the picturesque Pedro de Luna, Benedict XIII, fled, in his obstinacy, to the impregnable fortress of Pensacola in Spain, claiming until he died to be Peter's true successor. Had the council actually carried the day? One might have thought so when, in 1417, a canon was passed by the assembly making the Council an enduring institution in the Church, a sort of watch-dog over the Pope. But, as a matter of fact, with his rivals out of the way, the newly-elected Martin V successfully gained the upper hand and displayed great intelligence and forcefulness. Although permitting the calling together of minor councils to which the ecumenical title was not to be accorded, he set about re-establishing pontifical authority so that a new crisis would not again successfully challenge it.

A second crisis did occur during the stormy pontificate of Eugenius IV (1431-1437), and was, in large part, due to the blundering ways of that upright and pious Pontiff. He convoked the Council of Bâle—the very council whose right to be numbered among the ecumenical gatherings is so disputed —despite the resistance of bishops who at first refused to participate in it. He then flew in the face of the proponents of conciliar prejudices by dissolving the council. And then, after rescinding that order, he succeeded only in making a public show of the tragic rupture which divided the assembly from himself. On its part, Bâle proclaimed conciliar supremacy, condemned Eugenius IV as heretical because he would not subscribe to its own contentions and then heaped scandal upon scandal by electing in his place Amadeo, Duke of Savoy, as Felix V. Felix soon found the honor an insupportable burden. As a matter of fact, the fathers of Bâle (among whom there were but few cardinals and bishops) were not of much account. And, moreover, they were themselves blunderers. The crowned heads viewed with distaste their revolutionary and democratic tendencies, and, one after the other, rallied to the cause of Eugenius IV. The worthy Felix V was glad to resign in full sincerity. The papacy emerged victorious from this crisis, and Cardinal Torquemada brilliantly set forth, in his *Summa de Ecclesia,* the thesis of papal primacy.

Moreover, two ecumenical councils were destined to abet this victory of the papacy, the one by preparing and the other by confirming it. The first of these, opened at Ferrara and moved to Florence (1438-1445), under the mandate of Eugenius IV himself even before Bâle had ended, was the occasion of a papal triumph; for at it oriental Christians, in the person of the Emperor of Constantinople, the Patriarch, and many other Eastern Orthodox prelates, were content to overlook the difficulties which, in the eleventh century, had issued in the Greek schism. Thus the Church was again sealed in unity. This could be no more than provisional, but it, nevertheless, shed rays of glory round the Pope. And, in 1512, the Fifth Lateran Council, the last of those held during this troubled era, having been convoked by the war-like Julius II, had no greater significance than its sustaining of that Pontiff in the face of the designs which King Louis XII of France had formed in order once again to set the council against the Pope.

The basic interest of all these happenings lies in the way they resulted in the triumph of the papacy; for, looking back one cannot ascribe much credit to the council. In the doctrinal field, the battle against the heresy of Jan Hus and the later condemnation, however veiled, of Pomponazzi's rationalism; in the administrative field, some canons concerning episcopal appointments, the organisation of the religious congregations and the censorship of books. As far as concerns the larger reform, the necessity for which had precipitated the whole crisis, it goes without saying that in the midst of their quarrels the fathers had little time for it. So it was not by chance that it was in the very year, 1517, of the closing of the Fifth Council of the Lateran that Luther fastened to the doors of Wittenberg Church his famous *Theses*.

Yet, on the contrary, may it not be that the conciliar crisis was of greater significance? The Popes were no longer off-guard in respect to the conciliar system; and the theologians devoted to the pontifical primacy were even less so. The modern doctrine of councils was formulated largely by way of opposition to the conciliar theory.

There is no doubt that by declaring that he desires to renew "an age-old tradition" His Holiness John XXIII has wished, in his wisdom, to point out that this lesson of history has not been lost upon him.

9. THE SPECTACULAR COUNCIL: TRENT

IT TOOK another quarter of a century before the decision was taken to call a new council into session. It was not that the need of reform grew less; quite the contrary was the case. No serious attempt had been taken to remedy the growing and daily more apparent evil. The good intentions which had inspired the canons of the Fifth Council of the Lateran served only as further paving stones on the road to hell. But zeal for reform animated men whose intemperance and pride outran their sincerity and moved them to rely more on their own notions than on the authorities: such were Luther and Zwingli, and, soon afterward, Calvin. The mere fact that certain of these extremists who were impatient, as well, of the existing dogmatic structure, never ceased to talk of "the council," was enough to make the heads of the Church wary of the idea of calling one. One after another, Martin V, Pius II, Sixtus IV, and Julius II declared that all appeals to general councils were interdicted and invalid, and that those who should give utterance to them were to be dealt with by the Inquisition. Clement VII, who feared that a council might examine too closely the legitimacy of his own birth, favored as much delay as possible in the calling of such a gathering. A nuncio wrote: "All the world cries out for a council." Many of the sovereigns favored it. The Roman Curia held back. Did it fear that a reform of "the Church in both head and members" would touch too sharply its own interests? It was not only this. The curia knew well the immense difficulties that would have to be surmounted and the danger there would be in bringing together an assembly whose decisions would be held as of no avail by two-thirds of Christendom.

For things had come to that pass. The Protestant revolution had turned into a catastrophe. The ancient structure of the Church was crumbling under its blows. Then it was that the Popes grasped the fact that they must themselves embody the principle of the needfulness of reform which the rebels had hugged to them as if it were their own, and that they must make the council their own affair. The courageous Farnese, Paul III, set his hand to the task. A first attempt had been made unsuccessfully at Mantua and later at Vienne, but he did not lose heart and a dual preparation began in the arena of papal relations with the imperial and royal courts and in the drawing up of a list of questions which might suitably be studied. At length, on December 13, 1545, the duly convoked council was opened. The place chosen for its sittings was an unexpected one—Trent, a town of six thousand souls which had the double advantage of being under the protection of the emperor and of being conveniently accessible from Italy. The old Pope had won: he had made his dream come true. But he was not to see the conclusion of his enterprise, for that was eighteen years in the future.

Thus was brought about that Council of Trent which is marked in the history of the Church as being the most important of all the councils. Is this due to the number of the participating fathers? To answer requires consideration; for their number varied very greatly; at the time of the first session they were but few: four cardinals, four archbishops, one and twenty bishops, and about fifty theologians. In the closing sessions, however, more than two hundred snowy mitres could be seen. At some of the sessions there were not more than twenty fathers all told.

But the importance of this council rests in its characteristic marks. It was ecumenical in the sense that it was convoked in the prescribed manner by the Sovereign Pontiff and was accessible to all parts of the Catholic unity. It was simply and purely ecclesiastical, in spite of the intrigues of many of the lay powers to insure a hearing for their own preferences. It was composed solely of bishops and generals of religious orders, assisted in their labors by theologians they themselves had chosen. In its method of approach, it was most careful and wise. Every decision was arrived at after three stages of consideration: first of all, the points were "worked up" by theological committees; then the results were examined and voted upon by the general body of all prelates who had voting rights; finally, the decision was proclaimed in solemn session in the midst of impressive liturgic ceremonial.

It would be an understatement to declare merely that the work of the council was done under the papal eye: the ideas of

the Popes were continually and strictly linked to the deliberations. When a difficulty would arise, the pontifical legates—all
of whom were remarkable men—would sound an "alert" to
Rome, and soon there would arrive a platoon of bishops who
would cast the balance on the side of the discussion which was
most favored there. The wits of the council used to say: "See
how the Holy Spirit is coming to us in the Roman dispatch
boxes!" Only one Pope, the dreaded Paul IV, thought of going himself to the assembly so that by force of his decrees
he might single-handedly effect the reform of the Church
and spear-head the Counter-Reformation; but the designs of
Providence interfered with his plans. His successor, Pius IV,
made his chief concern the matter of bringing the council to
its term. This he did with the help of a saint, his nephew
Charles Borromeo. When, on December 4, 1563, the closing
session was held in the brilliantly illuminated cathedral of
Trent, the delirious cries of joy were a tribute not only to the
work of the council but to the patient efforts of the Popes.

Trent accomplished an enormous task. We are in a better
position to evaluate it than were its contemporaries; and this
is due to the *Acta* which have been published by the
learned German scholarly society called after Gorres, as well
as to the Roman periodical which has as its only aim the study
of Trent. Cardinal Hergenrother wrote: "No council in the
Church's history ever defined so many theses; none ever established so many doctrinal points nor made more laws." It
was an enormous and admirable work: after having so long
delayed, the Church now expressed, in vigorous and precise
terms, her reply to the contentions of heresy and to the criticisms which had been levelled at her. The council affirmed
the true doctrine, rooted alike in Scripture and in tradition,
which touches the whole field of belief, especially in reference
to the questions raised by Luther and Calvin concerning the
plan of salvation, grace, the Church's hierarchical structure,

and the nature of the sacraments; and the result showed that the contentions of the Reformers were only partially true. In disciplinary matters, the council enacted numerous regulations which, by putting an end to old aberrations, went far toward effecting that decisive transformation that has resulted in the Church we know. No pressing need—whether concerning the rights and duties of bishops or the education of priests in seminaries (determined upon in 1563), or the behavior of the people, or the rules about the administration of the sacraments or the use of the missal and breviary—was knowingly neglected by the council. The unmistakable result of the Tridentine assembly was a wonderful renewal of Catholicism; and there emerged from the council a Church more aware of itself, better established in dogmatic formulation, better fitted to govern souls. All this had its roots in the oft-times stormy sessions held in the little Alpine city. This was not, as has often been said, a new Church, but rather a Church with a new aspect.

This is not to say that one may have no reservations in estimating the worth of Trent; for it must at once be admitted that certain questions were actually slighted. Such was, for example, the problem of the Church's relationship to sovereign powers. Then again, it may be thought that the notable centralization of the Church, in which the Tridentine reform issued, has had as its consequence the encouragement of certain tendencies which have caused the misunderstanding of some precious facets of ecclesiastical tradition which had for long sanctioned an order of things owing quite as much to diversity as to hierarchical stability. More seriously even, the question whether the council, by aiming to set forth the elements of doctrine threatened by the disaffected, had not shown itself incapable of grasping the deepest reality at stake, the nature of the Church. As a matter of fact, it was precisely the theology of the Church which, after Trent, needed to be expressed. The obligation incumbent upon the council to face the attack from Protestantism has had another consequence: dogmatic definitions which emphasized points distinguishing Catholics from Dissenters have cast into the shade that area in which all are at one in faith and in Christ. It might be said that it is not a good thing to learn the catechism in order to use it against anyone. As we see the assembling of the council which His Holiness John XXIII has been inspired to call, we may recollect these two issues—the need for greater precision in respect to the theology of the Church, and the need of establishing relations with separated brethren.

10. VATICAN I: THE UNCOMPLETED COUNCIL

ONCE AGAIN, the years rolled by without any council being called. This time the interval was a long one, three hundred years. In the whole series of the councils there is no similar chronological hiatus to be noted in the listing of them. Did the Popes of these three centuries fear that another assembly might turn against them, or that the bishops would make of it a ground of anti-papal resistance, or perhaps that the secular powers who had, often enough, "a bone to pick with them" might make a council the excuse for undesired interference? It seems, at least, that they thought the Tridentine canons adequate in respect of all necessary questions and needing no more than a fresh interpretation in response to changing circumstances.

However, in the middle of the nineteenth century, the idea of holding a council did recommend itself to many minds, and chiefly to the mind of that great Pope, Pius IX. This was not because the Church was in a state of crisis or because there was needed a reform *in capite et in membris* as had been so much of a consideration in the sixteenth century. There were two determining reasons:

"Those who were opposed to the faith, whether they were rationalists, or atheists, or free-thinkers, occupied themselves with ceaseless attacks, of increasingly violent nature, against either the tenets or the traditional functioning of the Church. And, in addition, the world had changed because of the disappearance of the old political regimes, the vast challenge to apostolic work posed by colonial expansion, and the development of new nations and changed cultures, with all the novel problems to which these changes had given rise."

The task of the council would be to determine the place of the Church in the world to which the great revolution had given birth.

Pius IX knew the necessity of keeping abreast of the times. Giovanni-Maria Mastai-Ferratti, the one-time "liberal" Archbishop of Mantua, had more awareness of his own age than his adversaries credit him with. Nevertheless, he did not think it well to summon a general council before issuing his condemnation of modern errors and setting forth a list of them in his *Syllabus*, nor even—and this is more significant—when it was a matter of defining dogma, as he had done in respect to the Immaculate Conception of the Virgin Mary in 1854. The wish to see Papal Infallibility proclaimed, although it is over-stressed by many an historian, was not, therefore, the only—and, perhaps, not even the chief—motive in the mind of the Pope; for he had already made free use of this prerogative. Just before the publication of the *Syllabus* in 1864, he declared in private to the cardinals present in Rome that he was giving thought to convoking a council, that "an extraordinary measure" seemed to him necessary "to bind up the extraordinary wounds of the Church," then under attack from so many sides. The majority of those he consulted agreed with him, and so, too, did thirty-six bishops from various parts of the world whom he questioned some months later. This idea of Pius IX was strongly encouraged by the celebrated Bishop Dupanloup. It was disapproved only by certain Romans who, like Cardinal Pitra, feared and dreaded a council as something which might "turn things upside down." But Pius IX would brook no resistance, and on June 29, 1868, by the Bull *Aeterbi Patris* he called to Rome the representatives of ecumenical Christianity, setting the meeting for the Feast of the Immaculate Conception, December 8, 1869.

It seemed, from its very beginnings, that this Council of the Vatican was to be one of the most important in the Church's history. The right side of the transept of Saint Peter's Basilica was converted into a hall for the conciliar sessions, and here as many as 764 conciliar fathers could be seated, that is to say, three times more than the number who attended the best-attended of the Tridentine sessions. Hundreds of theologians and canonists prepared materials for the meetings, and the Eternal City was filled to overflowing with interested visitors and journalists on the alert for news. Thanks to the railroads, traveling had become easier; and the press, on the whole, underlined the importance of the council which was to mark, as Dupanloup had said, "a new dawn and not a setting sun."

It was primarily and exclusively a Church assembly. All the bishops had been invited, even those who were not ordinaries and who were then known as *episcopi in partibus infidelium.**

---

* That is to say, bishops assigned to sees *in infidel* (in the sense of being non-Christian) *lands*. This term was due to the fact that the title *bishop* has long been, basically, a territorial one, and every bishop must, according to long-established canonical practice therefore be designated as the chief shepherd of some definite geographical locality in the Church. When it became necessary or desirable, chiefly in order to supply assistant prelates charged with administrative or ceremonial detail or to honor favored or deserving ecclesiastics with high personal rank, to confer episcopal orders on men not charged with the personal obligation of governing a diocese committed to them, such prelates were given the designation of some extinct episcopal see of the early church, some territory wherein Christianity no longer flourished. Within the past century, this condition having changed

Also summoned were the presidents of monastic congregations and the superiors general of religious orders. But breaking sharply with immemorial custom, Pius IX had decided that the lay powers were not to be represented, and of this papal decision, Emile Olivier, speaking before the French Chamber of Deputies, had declared that it constituted "the separation of Church and state, effected by the Pope himself." All the great powers acquiesced in this decree of exclusion, even Napoleon III whose troops were actually protecting Rome at the time. After some reflection, he resigned himself to not exercising the right of sending an ambassador.

As a purely ecclesiastical assemblage, the Council of the Vatican was truly ecumenical. The five parts of the world enjoyed representation among the fathers, and this included Anglo-Saxon and Latin American countries which had not been participants in the sessions of Trent. There were, in addition, fifty orientals. If it had been up to the Pope alone, certain separated brethren would have been seated as delegates in this gathering of Christians. As a matter of fact, referring to the councils of Lyon and of Florence, Pius IX had sent an invitation to the Orthodox Greeks; but it had been brutally rejected. To the Protestants had been sent a brief which was not exactly a model of tact, and very few of them would have ventured to declare that the time seemed promising for an exchange of messages.

It must be added that the work of the council was prepared and even led in a much more determined fashion than had

---

and the territory of these old dioceses having been observed to be occupied again by Christians, even if not always by Christians in communion with Rome, the Holy See out of an unwillingness to offend these people by calling them *infidels*, has changed the curial usage, and the prelates in question are now termed *episcopi titulares* or titular bishops. It was in a similar spirit that the late Pope Pius XII ordered a change in the Roman Liturgy of Good Friday in which Christians are now called upon to pray for the Jews simply as *pro Judaeis* without the addition of the offensive adjective *perfidiis*. [Translator's note.]

been the case at Trent. That council had suffered from grave methodological defects, the rules and procedure having been, as it were, improvised by the papal legates to meet each circumstance as it arose. In the case of the Vatican Council, the Bull *Multiplices* prescribed a regimen which some found quite Draconian. This rendered impossible interminable discussions of the Tridentine type. Five carefully appointed and guided preparatory sub-commissions had prepared the way by establishing schedules as a basis for the work of the conciliar commissions. The Pope alone had the right of initiating matters. Projects suggested by the bishops themselves were given short shift unless the program committee took an interest in them. Four permanent committees drew up the actual texts of decress, something which had offered great opportunities for the wasting of time in past councils. Matters were then put to the vote before the general assembly, and were finally promulgated in solemn sessions. The whole procedure was thus quite definitely set, something which will not fail to be remembered at the Second Vatican Council.

If the results effected by the First Vatican Council are to be fairly judged, it must be borne in mind that this meeting, which seemed as important for the Church's future as Trent had been thought to be, was interrupted after one year's work, and was thus far from being able to study, much less to resolve, all the questions on the agenda. It was not the unfettered decision of the Church which brought the council to a close but rather the Piedmontese artillery. This explains that lack of balance in estimating the results of this council, a lack often remarked, and one engraven indeed on the pages of history when, in an effort at simplest expression, the First Council of the Vatican is described as "the council of Papal Infallibility."

Actually, the work of preparation had guaranteed the classification of the schedules into two main categories. One, under the rubric of Christian Doctrine, embraced matters concerned with resistance to the chief errors and heresies of the modern world; the other, under the rubric of The Church of Christ, permitted consideration of the whole question of the Church, its essential nature, its organisation, and its relationship with the secular powers. Actually, work on the first of these had been undertaken calmly and had led to a primary, if negative, result, in the condemnation of modern heresies. The study of the Church was soon dominated by one question which the preparatory commission had not even set down in the *schema* but which everyone was conscious of as being uppermost in all minds: this question concerned the primacy of the Pope and his infallibility.

It is known under what conditions and as a result of what discussions the solution reached the stage of formulation. Inasmuch as there were fifteen chapters in the *schema* entitled *De Ecclesia Christi* wherein only the question of the primacy of the Pope was posed in the eleventh and twelfth, the most confirmed partisans of the pre-eminent power of the papacy succeeded in giving this article priority in the discussion and in adding to it an addendum covering infallibility. To tell the truth, it was an irresistible current which guided the thought of the fathers into granting to the papacy augmented authority and prestige. It was so little to be resisted that the council suspended discussion when there were still forty of the fathers who desired to address it upon the subject. The forces of opposition were slight; for 451 votes of *placet* won an easy victory over 88 of *non placet* and 62 of *placet juxta modum.**
And when, on July 18, the new dogma was promulgated in solemn session, there were but two voices raised in negation, the remaining members of the opposition having preferred to leave the council early.

------

* That is to say, the ayes had it by 363 against those who voted no, and by 389 against those who desired an amended formulary. [Translator's note.]

The interruption, that autumn, of the conciliar sessions prevented the consideration of the *Schema De Ecclesia,* and the study of the other questions, serious and many as they were, which had been set forth on the agenda. The Council of the Vatican thus brought into high relief one part of the theological doctrine of the Church, but only one; leaving most patently to its successor in the future an obligation to bring its work to a conclusion. This is not the same as declaring, as certain intemperate critics have done, that the council was "abortive." In the dogmatic area there are accomplishments less spectacular which are worthy of being pondered. The constitution *Dei Filius* has established with precision the connection between reason and faith, and has paved the way for the revitalization of theological and scriptural study. It is in that constitution that one finds the definition of being and the demonstration of the importance of the signs of revelation which has bulked so large in making evident the identification of the Jesus of history and the Christ of faith. And, when the Vatican archives for this period are made fully available, it will take only one careful scholarly study to show what is owed by the theologians of the past century, and even the great papal encyclicals of that period, to the unsung toil of the commissions which prepared the *schema* which the council did not have the opportunity to put to the vote.*

11. IS THE COUNCIL WHOLLY UNEXPECTED?

ONCE THE FATHERS had returned home, once the violent agitation against infallibility by its most fervent opponents, Dolinger, Hyacinthe Loison, and the Old Catholics had failed,

---

* M. l'Abbe de Ladoue, who had gone with the Bishop of Frejus to Rome, pointed out that "Apart from the great matter of infallibility, I do not believe that the Council of the Vatican will be able to put into effect any reforms. Men's minds are not prepared and means are wanting."

the council seemed rapidly to pass out of memory. Thought of the old Pope, "the prisoner of the Vatican," disturbed men more than all the questions which the interruption of the conciliar sittings have left in a state of suspense. Theoretically, the council was not yet over; at a moment's notice, on the mandate of the Pope, the sessions could be resumed; but, actually, it seemed unthinkable that the council would come together again in a city subjected to an excommunicated king and under the leadership of a Pontiff who himself declared that he was not free. Even Leo XIII, so courageous in his policies, so little inclined to docile conformity, did not dream of it. Indeed, he undoubtedly never felt it would be necessary to call about himself an assembly whose outlook could not be guaranteed to coincide with his own.

So it was that, to the Romans, "the council" no longer suggested that general assembly of the Church which might, some day or other, again occupy an arm of the transept of Saint Peter's; it rather signified that Congregation of the Council which had been founded by Pius IV in 1564 with the intent of keeping careful surveillance over the true interpretation and the due implementation of the Tridentine decrees, and into whose hands Pius X had entrusted "the general governance of the diocesan clergy and Christian people" in all matters other than those which referred to the episcopate or the sacraments. This body is, in effect, a dicastery—a kind of court of justice —or, one might say, a ministry of the interior occupied with the setting of feats and fasts, with keeping an eye on rectors of parishes, on canons, on pious associations and confraternities, with the settlement of financial questions in respect to bequests, with Mass stipends and with the appropriation of the temporalities of the Church, and finally with the settlement of conflicts about parish lines.

Among all these functions, only one recalls its original importance, and that is the right which the Congregation of the

Council enjoys to act in all matters having reference to the councils of the past or the future, and, by consequence of this, in all meetings of the episcopate. The announcement, in 1959, has therefore evidently resulted in directing the work of this Roman congregation along lines more in keeping with its original objective.

It appears, however, that the idea of the council as a Church assembly seems to have had small place in the minds of Catholics. It is noteworthy that of the dozen studies which have appeared during the past fifteen years on the papacy and its organization not one has marked the council as being an institution of the Church, even those theologians who regretted the interruption which prevented the Vatican Council from finishing its work and who deplored the fact that, as Msgr. Carton de Wiart, Bishop of Tournai, puts it, "the definition of Papal Infallibility has distracted attention from and has cast into the shade" some significant matters, including those which bear upon the duties of the episcopate, have not, in any manner whatsoever, inferred that conciliar session should be renewed within the halls of the Vatican.

Is this to say that no one has given any thought to a council? Pius XI showed that he had. His first encyclical, *Ubi Arcano Dei*, contained an avowal that he would not shrink from "setting himself, forthwith to the re-opening of the ecumenical council" which had been able to bring to a conclusion no more than one point, however great its importance, of its agenda. He awaited "some clearer manifestation of God's will." However, he did sponsor a deeper study of the *Acta* of the Vatican Council, entrusting it to a commission of theologians and canonists, even suggesting to them the point of considering whether he ought to close Vatican I and think of Vatican II or decree a continuation of the assembly suspended in October, 1870. A leading professor at the Angelicum, the French Dominican, Père Hugon, gave special attention to this matter. Nevertheless, even when the settlement of the Roman question had been effected by the conciliatory Accord between the Italian state and the Vatican, Pius XI did not proceed beyond these preliminary approaches.

In his turn, Pius XII gave some thought to the council. Cardinal Tardini, in the panegyrical discourse in memory of the late Pope which he delivered on October 20, 1959, reported that he had commissioned "a group of learned ecclesiastics" to work toward the eventual convocation of a council. And the Archbishop of Palermo, Cardinal Ruffini, related that, as early as 1939, when he had suggested to the then-new Pontiff that circumstances seemed to him to require the convocation of a council at least as urgently as in the days which had preceded Trent, Pius XII welcomed the suggestion and "took a note of it, as he was accustomed to do in respect to all important matters." As a matter of fact, he did not neglect the notion inasmuch as he caused Cardinal Costantini to draw up a *schema* of two hundred pages on the problem of the unity of Christians, a *schema* which he planned to have brought before the council.

Despite all this, the council seemed a far-off thing until 1958. It was not because there were wanting Catholics who, like Cardinal Ruffini, felt that the condition of the times was of sufficient seriousness to make necessary the calling of an ecumenical assembly. It is true that the Church was not in the grip of any such interior crisis as had led to the convocation of Trent, it was no longer a question of suggesting a reform *in capite et in membris*. But it was beyond question that the world had moved on, that it had changed perhaps even more since 1870 than during the three hundred years which lay between the Council of Trent and the Council of the Vatican. Was it not necessary, once again, that the Church be brought up to date in organization, in methods of fulfilling its mission, in the development of its intellectual life? If it be true that, as Msgr. Jager, Archbishop of Paderborn—one of those who has made most clear the roots and the meaning of Vatican II—has declared, "councils are always held at the great crossroads in the Church's history," it is evident that the Christian world now faces one such turning point.

Such are the circumstances under which, at the beginning of his pontificate, His Holiness John XXIII has made public his resolution to summon an ecumenical council. There can be no doubt that he is deeply aware of the need of the Church to set forth the problems which face it and to find a solution to them. As a diplomat of long experience, as the head of a great diocese he knows very well that there are problems which cannot be passed over. But why has the infallible Pontiff chosen to have recourse to a council rather than to act on his sole responsibility? There can be no doubt that the humility which is among the most evident of his personal characteristics is at least partially the reason for this decision, but it is due, as well, to his deep conviction—one that he has frequently expressed—that, now, more than ever, the Church must function a community, as a fraternity which is *at unity with itself*.

It may be asked whether that sudden insight to which, again humbly, His Holiness John XXIII has ascribed the decision which he has taken, has not been prepared for, as is natural to so large-minded a man, by antecedent thought, by that kind of soul-searching which opens the way for the entry of God's grace. We shall see at once that, as early as 1953, the question of unity has been in the forefront of his thoughts—that unity to which, on January 25, 1959, he linked his decision to convoke a council. It is known, on the other hand, that during his lifetime he has given much by way of learning, time, and financial support to the publication of the works of St. Charles Borromeo who was himself so deeply concerned with the final achievements of the Tridentine

Council. Finally, in its issues of May 1, 1957, and June 1, 1958, an Italian periodical, *Palestra del Clero*, drew the attention of its readers to the reasons which could lead to the convocation of an ecumenical council. *Palestra del Clero*, which is published at Rovigo is the organ of the clergy of the province of Veneto, and, at that time, the Patriarch of Venice was Cardinal Roncalli.

II

What is an Ecumenical Council?

———◆●◆———

1. "IT HAS SEEMED GOOD TO THE HOLY SPIRIT"

AT THE First Vatican Council, in that great meeting hall which had been made of the transept of Saint Peter's, the bishops, seated in eight rows arranged like steps, as well as the consultors and the guests of honor massed in the tribunes, could all see, on a central platform, a throne upon which a magnificent Bible had been placed. The opening session, at which they had assisted, had been conducted with great majesty, in the style of more solemn papal functions, with Pius IX presiding in person, and according to ceremonial forms which had scarcely changed from the days of the Council of Vienne (1311-1312). The coming deliberations of the Council were placed under the guidance of the Holy Spirit by the chanting of the *Veni Creator* and some other prayers. In this way the Church shows that by setting forth and promulgating decrees bearing upon the faith and conduct of Christians, it is fulfilling something religious in nature, an act of worship offered to God. It is by its liturgical aspect that the council is seen to differ radically from any parliamentary assemblage, despite some external points of resemblance.

Actually, an ecumenical council is not the parliament of the Church; it is not a meeting of elected representatives who have received a mandate from the people. It is true, indeed, that the participating bishops represent the people of their charge, but this is not in the same sense in which a deputy represents the electors. It is rather because each bishop is, in a sense, the incarnation of the Church which has been committed to him and which, in him, is summed up, according to the doctrine expressed by the great bishop of Carthage, Saint Cyprian, in the formulary, *Ecclesia in episcopo.** The binding link is a natural and not a political one, and there is nothing democratic about the delegation of the bishop's power.

An ecumenical council is emphatically not a constituent assembly such as that held in the United States in 1787, in order to establish the Constitution, the fundamental law of the land, according to new norms, following upon the Revolution. The Church knows that her constitution is not one which has been conceived by men: it has been given her by Christ; and no essential note of it can be changed either by the Pope or by the most solemn of assemblies. All that may be done to it is confined to renewal of means and methods by the enactment of laws which must be worked out in accordance with the teaching of tradition.

And, finally, least of all is an ecumenical council an international assembly of the kind which our own age has seen multiply with varying degrees of satisfaction, even though the delegates may be wearing devices which guarantee that all hear at one time. Although, by recruitment, the conciliar

---

* This formulary has, at times, been the cause of some discussion as though it reflected on the Roman primacy. It is clear that it is not taken in this sense today.

assembly is international, it is one in its nature. As each father of the council begins to play his role in it, he ceases to be part of any national or ethnic group; he is solely attached to the cause of God and of His Church. The decisions taken by the council do not derive, as in the United Nations, from the resolutions made by a majority of separate sovereignties: they embody the will of the Church which is one and universal. The will of this assembly can be expressed by ballot; it is, nonetheless, the will of a single entity having but one will.

All this amounts to saying—and I may be excused for recalling it—that the ecumenical council is an assembly of the Church, that is to say, of a society made up of men and having a government, laws, and institutions as earthly societies do, but a society which itself conceives of and defines itself as being transcendent and directed toward other ends than the mere good administration of the collective interest and the promotion of temporal well-being among its members. This is why the Holy Spirit is invoked at the opening of the conciliar sessions, for He is taken to be the one who inspires the decisions that are arrived at. This is why the council is, as we shall see, infallible; for the Holy Spirit preserves it from all error and makes of it, as of every aspect of the Church, that "pillar and foundation of truth" of which Paul tells us in his letter to Timothy. This turning toward the Third Person of the Trinity is definite and constant. No council in all history has failed to do this. And already, at the time of the "protocouncil" of Jerusalem in the year 49 or 50, the Apostles had explicitly so expressed themselves. After its decisions had been arrived at, in a letter written to the brethren of other communities, which the book of *Acts* preserves for us, we find a little phrase full of meaning: "It has seemed good to the Holy Spirit and to us . . . ." It is in accordance with the same line of thought that, on numerous occasions, when speaking

of the council which he has initiated, John XXIII has made
use of the word "Pentecost." For every council is a manifestation of the Holy Spirit.

If what has already been said of the basic Christian concept
of God's presence in united brethren be recalled, it will be
understood why the councils are always said to be "assembled
in the Holy Spirit." The oldest texts that we possess for the
reconstruction of the history of the councils show that the
words of Saint Matthew's Gospel, "Whenever two or three
are gathered together in my name, there am I also" have been
tirelessly repeated in discourses and sermons delivered during
the sessions. On the eve of the Council of Ephesus in 431, Pope
Symmachus wrote: "The priestly gathering sets forth the
presence of the Holy Spirit."

Every council also clearly manifests those social aspects
rightly marked in Catholicism by Père de Lubac: he infers
from these facts "that besetting outlook of mankind on the subject of unity," just as Canon Masure discerns it in the Gospels.
It is quite striking that it has often been the most strong-handed
of Popes, like Innocent III and Pius IX, whose authority was
not questioned by Catholics, who have desired to bring around
them representatives of the entire Church. By contrast, no
council can ever be regarded as being the work of any single
man. It is more than interesting to note that, whenever the
Church assembled in council at a time when it might have
been openly dominated by some powerful personality, that
personality was, either voluntarily or providentially, out of
touch with the assembly. Saint Augustine was dead when
there came to his door the autograph rescript of the emperor
which commanded him to go to the Council of Ephesus in 430;
Saint Thomas Aquinas died on the journey to the Council of
Lyon in 1274; Saint Bernard, who was law-giver to all Europe
in his day, did not attend the Council of the Lateran which, in

1139, put an end to the schism of Anacletus, that schism which the great monk had done so much to combat.

In the fullest sense of the word, the council is the gathering together of the Church, the gathering together of the assembly of the Christian community. And the conditions under which the council comes together will not be understood unless it be recalled how the Church defines itself and into what framework it sets its fellowship.

2. "ECUMENICAL"

THE TERM "ecumenical" is ambivalent and disputed. In Greek, *oikumenos* means the inhabited earth, the whole of the known world. It was the boast of Rome that it had unified the known world under its rule; and Rome came near to doing that. In the official language of the later Empire *oikumenos phay* was conceived of as being synonymous with *imperium romanum,* and for this reason the councils convoked by the emperors and drawing representatives from all over the empire were said to be *ecumenical.* In reference to the Council of Nicea, Saint Athanasius said: "The fathers have come from every part of the *oikumenos.*"

In the grammatical, exact, and precise sense of the word, *ecumenical* then should mean *universal.* As a matter of fact no ecumenical council has ever been universal in the sense that it numbered among its fathers representatives of every race and nation without distinction of religion, and including even pagans. The general councils of the Middle Ages were even less universal in this sense than were the "ecumenical" councils of the Orient; and this is still more true of Trent and the Vatican. As an assembly of the Church the council is not, and could never be, an international conference where rival beliefs confront each other. Even if Protestant Christians or Eastern Orthodox Christians should come to it, their presence would not change its essential character.

In this area confusion is possible and frequent with reference to the *ecumenical movement* developed by the World Conference on Faith and Order, especially since 1919, among the different branches of Protestantism. Anglicanism and even Eastern Orthodoxy has collaborated, and this has led to the setting up of the World Council of Churches whose meetings, especially those following the one held at Amsterdam in 1948, have attracted much attention. By definition, in these assemblies the differing kinds of Christianity can be represented, and they share equal rights. Yet one might remark that even this ecumenicism is no more universal than that of the councils since the inhabited world is not fully represented, nor are either Buddhists or Moslems to be encountered at the sittings. But, in any case, this is a concept wholly different from that of the Church. Whatever may be the sympathetic interest which Catholics can feel for all strivings after unity, the ecumenical movement is something wholly different from the ecumenical council.

The universality of the council is the universality of the Church. It has spread out into every part of the world, and it is the Catholics who come from all these regions who represent the whole world at the council. Consequently, before a council can be considered to be ecumenical, all the representatives of the Catholic world, that is to say all the bishops, shall have been officially summoned. And, furthermore, they must attend in sufficient numbers so that this Catholic world will seem to be visibly represented.

"But," as Forget writes in the *Dictionnaire de Théologie Catholique*, "since it is clearly impossible that all bishops actually can come, it is evident that the quality of ecumenicity cannot be based upon the effective participation of all or of almost all. It is not even required that the number of those present exceed the absentees. The history of several councils which are, beyond question, ecumenical—and Trent is an example—is alone enough to prove that. How many bishops must be present to constitute a quorum? Neither theology nor Canon Law offer a categorical and generally applicable reply to this query. But here is, at the least, a general indication: following upon the universal convocation, there ought to be at the actual meeting bishops or prelates from different countries in such number and variety that, having due regard to the circumstances, one can, speaking truly and morally, say that the assembly really constitutes a representation of the whole Church. In the case of serious doubt about the ecumenicity of this or that council, the Church itself has the right peremptorily to settle this question of dogmatic fact."

"The numbers have nothing to do with the case," as we find Bossuet writing to Leibniz. No more, he adds, than does the overwhelming predominance of bishops from one country—to be particular, Greeks, at first, and then, later, Italians —which has marked certain of the councils. "Despite the fact that the Italians outnumbered us at Trent," as the eagle of Meaux justly remarks, "they did not thereby dominate us: we are all of one faith."

The ecumenicity of the councils, then, is definitively linked to the notion which the Church has of its own unity, and to the Catholic principle of the collective infallibility of the college of shepherds, united to the Pope, who are heirs of the Apostles and, like them, depositories of the divine gospels. This conception, which is at the same time "communitarian" and hierarchical, finds in the Pope its height and its fulfillment; and this is why the role of the Vicar of Christ is, in respect to the council, a fundamental one.

3. POPE AND COUNCIL

IN THE CHAPTER of the code of Canon Law which is concerned with ecumenical councils, insistence is laid upon this determining role of the Pope. "An ecumenical council cannot be had lacking convocation by the Roman Pontiff," declares canon 222. "It is the right of the Roman Pontiff to preside at the ecumenical council, in his own person or by delegate; it is he who establishes and decides on the matters which are to be taken up and in what order; it is he who can transfer the council to another locale; he can suspend it or dissolve it, and he can confirm its decrees." And canon 229 repeats even more forcefully this final point with the precise declaration: "The decrees of the council have definitive obligatory force only after they have been confirmed by the Roman Pontiff and promulgated by his order."

This tells us to what degree a council may be the work of one Pope. It is quite legitimate to describe the First Council of the Vatican as "the Council of Pius IX," just as, in every sense, the Second Vatican Council has been known, since its announcement, and will be known in history, as "the Council of John XXIII." The ecumenical gathering together of the Church is knit to the person of the Pontiff to such a degree that, doubtless in order to avoid all danger of schism, or rather than risk a derangement of procedure, canon 229 establishes that the council is *ipso facto* interrupted in case the Pope should die. In such a case, his successor has the right to reconvene it, should he judge it good to do so.

Such is the state of the present legislation. The history of the councils demonstrates that the conditions which the code today lays down were not always respected. Were not the first eight councils convoked by the emperors? Neither political opinion nor the bishops stood out against this, and the Popes themselves suffered the sovereigns to exercise a right of the papacy. The response may, of course, be made that almost always the Popes approved, even advised, the convocation of the council and then either assisted at it or sent legates, and they confirmed its decisions. The case of the First Council of Constantinople in 381 is highly indicative of the authority which the Roman Pontiffs held in regard to the council. Convoked by the Emperor Theodosius without any previous agreement with Pope Damasus who was not even represented at it, this council was never recognised by the West as being ecumenical until much later when, in the sixth century, Popes Vigilius, Pelagius II and Gregory Magnus declared its decrees authoritative On the other hand, the Westerners would not grant the validity of the clause in the *Credo* concerning the Holy Spirit which had been voted by the council, except by interpreting the formulary as meaning "proceeding from the Father *and* the Son," whereas the orientals understood it to mean "issuing from the Father *by* the Son." We know that this is that *Filioque* destined to become a stone of offense between the Churches of East and West.

The Roman Pontiff's role is, then, a decisive one in everything which concerns the ecumenical council. It is even so decisive that some have asked if his intervention at every stage of the assembly's existence does not make any assembly either meaningless or useless. In his *appeal to the Nobles of Germany*, Luther came quickly to this conclusion. And immediately after the proclamation of papal infallibility, Dollinger, as we have already seen, was of the same opinion.

Great as may be the authority of the infallible Pontiff, the council remains, close to his side and a significant force among the institutions which foster the life of the Church. It is not by chance that the canons of the code which refer to the council are placed immediately after those which concern the papacy, and preceding those which have to do with the cardinalate. What then is the usefulness of an ecumenical council? Is it only in order to surround the Pontiff with glory, as has happened often enough in past times, as, for instance, in the cases of Innocent III and Pius IX? This will be part of its function, but not the whole of it. But, as we have seen, when brought together in circumstances which the Church finds difficult or which require that decisions be taken, an ecumenical council can bring to the aid of the infallible *magisterium* (the Church's teaching authority) the support which derives from collective thought, from general experience. It is because of this that we can call it true collaboration.

An historical example suffices to show how this kind of collaboration can be set up and what kind of climate of reciprocal confidence it requires. In the middle of the fifth century, the Church found itself face to face with the monophysite heresy which taught that in Christ there is but one nature. The convocation of an ecumenical council seemed advisable, and this was done at Chalcedon in 451. The Emperor Marcian wrote to the Pope, Saint Leo Magnus, telling him of his wish to call a council and suggesting that the Pope serve as an honorary chairman. The Pope replied immediately that he would actually preside by sending two of his legates. At the same time he addressed to the Patriarch the celebrated *Epistola ad Flavium* in which he himself treated of the mystery of the Incarnation in a way which steered clear of all erroneous notions. This letter was read in the council and it aroused much enthusiasm among the six hundred assembled fathers, one of whom cried out: "Peter has spoken through Leo." Nevertheless, the fathers continued their work, using the papal document as its basis. On their part, the papal legates made no objection to a collective effort being undertaken so that even more clarity and precision could be added to the pontifical statement and the danger of any false interpretation of it minimised. Finally, the formulary as voted upon was sent to Saint Leo. He pronounced it to be perfect and a better statement than his original. Thus did he approve the decisions of the council. This is a fine example of collaboration.

And, moreover, when one studies the work of the committees and the *Acta* of the Council of Trent in those learned volumes which the Gorres Society has issued, one realizes that these remarkable texts owe to the collaboration of many different theologians their precision and, at the same time, their truly "catholic" breadth and inclusiveness. This is not something which one man, assisted only by reticent subordinates, could have done.

Cardinal Cajetan made the profound observation that, in respect to its intensive nature, the authority of the Pope is equal to that of the council, but insofar as concerns its concrete fullness, its extensive nature, this is not so. This conception is rooted in the notion of the Church as a society which is a true community, a notion fully evangelical, recalling the words of Saint Matthew's Gospel (XVIII, 20), for it is in the coming together of faithful souls that Christ is in their midst, as He has promised. At the opening of the constitution *Dei Filius*, voted by the same Vatican which proclaimed Papal Infallibility, one reads, in reference to the ecumenical council: "It is in it that the holy principles of religion are more fully defined, are expressed with increased fullness; in it is ecclesiastical discipline restored and more soundly established so that the members are rejoined to their head, whence flows the strength of the entire mystical body of Christ."

If one had to prove that the council is not useless, these words would do it well.

4. "BISHOPS COMPOSE THE COUNCIL"

How IS THE council made up? Who are they who have a right to membership? The two hundred twenty-third canon of the code answers this question: "The following are summoned to the council and enjoy in it the right of deliberation: the cardinals, even though they be not bishops; patriarchs, primates, archbishops, residential bishops (that is, those who are charged with the responsibility of governing a diocese), even though they be still awaiting consecration; abbots *nullius* and prelates *nullius* (that is, responsible directly to Rome and charged with jurisdiction over a group of the faithful); abbots who are superiors of monastic congregations, superiors general of orders of priests. Titular bishops enjoy also the right of deliberation unless it be otherwise provided in the terms of convocation. Theologians and canonists who may be invited to the council enjoy only the right of consultation."

A list like this shows the breadth of these meetings. Following upon the announcement of the new council, a quick estimation, later confirmed by an official announcement of the number of prelates consulted prior to the assembly, sets as a probable figure for those who will attend it a number in excess of 2800, although, at the First Vatican Council, there were only about a thousand present.

All who actually receive a summons to the council are absolutely obliged to attend it. Every bishop swears, in the oath which he takes prior to being consecrated, that he will, among other things, come to take his seat in a council should he be called to do so. And, as one prelate jokingly said, "As if to put a premium on virtue, the code of Canon Law provides that the months which are passed outside a man's diocese while he is sitting in the council are not to be reckoned as part of the vacation to which he is entitled each year!"

It goes without saying that not every bishop is able to obey the order of convocation: age or illness or political considerations prevent some from doing so. At the First Vatican Council there were three hundred absentees out of a thousand who had been invited. Should it be absolutely impossible for anyone summoned to the council to attend it, he may designate a representative, although he may not delegate power to vote in his stead. And, of course, no father of the council may retire from the assembly without the permission of the president.

In our day, participation in the council, which is at one time the sign of its necessity and the guarantee of its ecumenicity, scarcely raises any of the special problems which marked the first nineteen of the councils in times when journey afoot, on horseback, in carriages, or by boat, were always more or less adventures. It took months and months to reach the place of meeting. For example, the Portuguese bishop, Barthélemy des Martyrs, left his city of Braga on March 24, 1561 and did not arrive at Trent until the following May 18, after a wearisome journey, which, however, in no wise diminished his combativeness. On his return from the same council, Perez de Ayala had to tarry for almost a month in the Balearic Isles for fear of storms and pirates.

Political affairs can also serve to dampen the zeal of those who would participate in the council. The most picturesque such example occurred at Easter in 1241, when the navy of Emperor Frederick II stopped the Genoese fleet, which had brought to their city more than one hundred fathers of a council convoked by Gregory IX. Frederick imprisoned all these distinguished personages. This was responsible for Innocent IV's decision to convoke the Council at Lyon, in imperial territory but close to France, where the archbishop was a temporal prince and practically independent. At the present time, the railroads and airplanes will make traveling more comfortable and swifter, but political considerations still bulk large as deterrents. At the first Council of the Vatican, practically all the bishops of dioceses located in the territories of the Tsar were absent, and when the Second Vatican Council was announced everyone wondered about the Church of Silence.

According to the list of members as given above from the code of Canon Law, it is evident that the council is indeed a meeting of bishops, something it has not always been throughout history. It is they alone, the shepherds of dioceses who are members of the council by divine right, by nature, and without the need of justifying their presence by referring to any canon or decree. Others have a right to a seat only on the strength of custom, or because of their own dignity, or because they, somehow, share in the jurisdiction proper to a bishop. The episcopal character is an essential prerequisite in anyone who would sit in an assembly of the teaching and governing Church. Archbishop Roberts, the former Archbishop of Bombay, who nobly resigned not long ago to make way for a native prelate (the future Cardinal Gracias), and whose spicy language frequently adds point to the truth, has summed up this canonical principle in these words, "A general council is a football match at which all the players are bishops."

Why this restriction to the bishops? It is theology which tells us. The bishops are *testes fidei,* witnesses to the faith of their flocks, *doctores fidei,* constituent members of the teaching Church, and *judices fidei,* judges competent to decide any question concerning faith. And it is to exercise this triple function that they come together in council. In truth, the particular and proper place which they occupy in the council and the role which they play in it cannot be understood except in the light of that *theologia episcopi,* that theology of the episcopal office which is too little known, even by Catholics. Too often the bishop is thought of—and perhaps insofar as France is concerned, this goes back to the Napoleonic concept of the nature of the Church—as a sort of state official, a prefect, who dresses in purple, and who is charged with the government of men and the superintendency of affairs, even though, speaking on the practical plane, the serious nature of the tasks entrusted to bishops should indicate how little this conception corresponds, on any fair reading of the matter, to a just notion of the essential nature of the episcopal office. It is not really any truer to say, as is frequently done, that the bishop is "the Pope's representative"; for this is a proper description of the papal nuncio or the apostolic delegate. Although the bishop depends on the Pope for his nomination, once he is designated and consecrated, he partakes of and shares in that *charisma*—that special gift of the Spirit—which makes of him, in the midst of the flock committed to him, *the* representative of Christ to them.

The bishops are the successors of the Apostles. This the Council of Trent has declared by describing them as "mainsprings of the hierarchical order, set by the Holy Spirit for the governance of the Church of God." Canon 229 of the code repeats this in specifying that it is "by divine institution" that they are "commissioned to head particular churches." Many of the Popes have confirmed this, as did Leo XIII when he declared the bishops to be "inheritors of the ordinary (or teaching and governing) power of the Apostles." This is the source of their powers. In a sense bishops share in the rights which the Twelve had because they had received the Gospel from Christ Himself so that they were, as Saint Paul tells us, the foundation stones of the Church. They have more to do than to be governors in the hierarchical society of the

Church; they are not merely the shepherds of the flock committed to them. They are witnesses to uninterrupted tradition, they are the agencies through which Christ ceaselessly pours grace upon those who worship Him; they are the ordinary ministers of the Sacrament of Confirmation; they are the living and numerous proof of the catholicity and the universality of the Church, for the whole episcopate is one, even though it extends all over the world.

Such definitions of the episcopate indicate why a council is something different than any lay assembly, and also why it is that the bishops are the only ones to sit in it. The traditional expression, *concilio esse episcoporum*, bishops compose the council, has not only a juridical, but also a mystical, sense in the magnificent perspective which Pius XII suggested in his celebrated encyclical on the Mystical Body, an encyclical which is among the major documents of his pontificate.

And it is because they are the heirs of the Apostles that the bishops assembled in council are able to make decisions which go far beyond, in scale and in extent of reference, anything which as individuals they might have in mind. We are aware, even in our own age, of bishops who have undertaken projects of great importance or who have published texts which stand out in religious history. Such, for example, is Cardinal Mercier who undertook, in company with Lord Halifax, conversations aimed at eventual reunion with the Anglican Church; such, again, is Cardinal Pie in his denunciation of modern error even prior to the *Syllabus*; and such, indeed, is Cardinal Suhard in having given us a diagnosis not likely to be improved upon of the state of the Church in the twentieth century. But all these projects, all these statements, become of universal value and worth only after the assembly of the Church has, as it were, rethought them and turned them to its own account. Just as it was to the Apostolic College that there was given the duty of guarding the sacred deposit of faith, so is it "to the episcopate alone," of which Saint Cyprian speaks, to the whole episcopal order, that there is entrusted the duty of furthering that faith. It is as a "pastoral corporation," and one—be it well understood—united to the Apostolic See, that the bishops function in the council.

Are there degrees in the pastoral corporation? Do all the conciliar fathers enjoy the same rights, are all of equal importance? In a gathering of many hundred members can the voice of the bishop of some small Italian diocese or that of a missionary bishop whose field of endeavor and whose theological and practical knowledge may be as circumscribed as are his territorial responsibilities, be raised as bravely as that of the cardinals who hold the great sees of Paris or New York? Speaking canonically, speaking theologically, a firm answer can be given: insofar as they are inheritors of the Apostles, all bishops are equal. But, in a practical case, so long as it is a matter of finding solutions to concrete problems, it is evident that those who have had some direct experience in the question at hand have a greater chance of influencing the decisions. It must not be forgotten, moreover, that in a council—just as in any other meeting—personal talent will cause some men to stand out from their fellows, talent, and that natural authority, that ability, that ease in discourse which makes one effective in a discussion. So it was at the First Vatican Council that certain fathers took a part greater than the importance of their sees alone would justify. This is true not only of the celebrated orator, Bishop Dupanloup, but also of the capable Bishop Mermillod of Geneva, and of the energetic Bishop Martin of Ratisbon, as well as of the ebullient Croat, Bishop Strossmayer, who lived in a place, Diakovar, that many members of the assembly would have been hard put to find if they were required to locate it on the map.

5. WHAT OF THE LAITY?

THE LAY CATHOLIC who looks at the manner in which an ecumenical council is organized may be tempted to conclude that this majestic assembly is no concern of his, at least insofar as concerns the making of the decisions which will be taken and which he, nonetheless, may have to incorporate into his life and conduct. To put it in a nutshell, the difference between the teaching Church and the Church taught will seem to him to be on this point, as on others, a very marked one indeed. Is there a real basis for this idea? Is the council none of the laity's business?

The reply to this question is more subtle and less simple than might appear at first glance. In the formal sense, laymen have no right of intervention in the council. And, as a matter of fact, ever since the conciliar crisis of the fifteenth century, they have not even had a place there. If, at Trent, a certain kind of lay influence was brought to bear upon the council, it was that of princes; and it was external, rather on the political than on the theological plane. Moreover, it was not very extensive. At the First Council of the Vatican, it must be recorded that there was neither any intervention on the part of the powers nor any lay members present among the fathers. The clerical character of the assembly was absolute and unmixed.

However, in the more or less official commentaries, just as in the more or less officious ones, to which the announcement of the convocation of a council by John XXIII has given rise, there is to be noted a certain insistence upon the fact that this event is of considerable interest to laymen also, and that they are associated with it. The arguments in favor of this fall under three heads.

To begin on the theological plane, we may note that Archbishop Bezelaire of Chambery, France, has stated at the head of one of his books, "The laity are also part of the Church," thus closely paralleling a formulary of Saint Avitus. Archbishop Jaeger of Paderborn has said:

> The episcopacy of the Church is closely united to the community of the faithful. The bishops, in conjunction with this community, form an organic body which cherishes and manifests Christian truth. They who teach the faith are, at the same time, of the faithful who profess the same faith to which all the faithful are witnesses in putting their belief into practice and in living Christian lives . . . It is not only the official teaching by the bishops of a valid and authentic faith, but, as well, the general and continued practice of that faith by Christians which gives testimony of truth . . . Great significance attaches, therefore, to the testimony of the believing people. It is a second witnessing of the Church's tradition.

In consequence, by virtue of the mere fact that he is a member of the faithful flock, in communion with his bishop and with the whole hierarchy of the Church, the layman is to be thought of as being associated with the work of the council and as participating in it indirectly, in a spiritual sense, just as he participates in the gifts of Pentecost.

It is, moreover, evident—and here is presented an argument on a second plane—that the mass of the faithful, even though they are actually absent from the council's deliberations, yet affect them. What is known in political language as public opinion is not wholly ineffective, even in the domain of religion. It is beyond question that on many occasions in the past it was at the wish of the laity that the calling of a council was pursued, and it was their wish as well which set the goal toward which the council was to work. It was, for example, the *vox populi* which, by engendering reform, had, in large measure, made certain that the Council of Trent would be held. Certain great issues whose resolutions stem rather from canonical procedures than from spiritual re-birth could never be solved at all had not the mass of the faithful agreed to co-operate. The matter of unity, of reconciliation with separated brethren, is one such question; and one must take into account that it was the Greek laity as much as the Greek clergy who categorically refused to accept the union which had been decided on at the Council of Florence in 1439 by the leading ecclesiastics of the Eastern Orthodox Church.

A third kind of participation by laymen at the council can be thought of in conjunction with work of an intellectual nature. Although the assembly is placed under the protection of the Holy Spirit, the matters with which it deals are the concern of men, their ideas and their way of life. This is as much as to say that, in given cases, the laymen who live out the problems are better acquainted with them—and in any case know them from a different situation—than can be the case with clerics. They are able, therefore, to supply to the fathers of the council documentation and useful suggestions. One of the best of the Roman theologians who have treated of the matter of the council, Father Spiazzi, a Dominican, observes that "the Church is present at the council in the person of theologians and other specialists—and this does not exclude laymen as such—who, although not part of the teaching and deliberating body, nevertheless make a contribution to it by their wishes and their advice (which can be of major importance in the consultive and scientific field). Insofar as action and human causality of it are concerned these may be determining in the council's work." These words are worthy of being underlined; their learned author was by no means writing in air.

In a practical sense laymen may function on two planes even if it be clear that they cannot participate in the sittings. They may, first of all, be consulted by their bishops who wish to do so before those prelates go forth to play their roles as *testes fidei,* witnesses of the faith. They may also be called to sit on the commissions which prepare the schedules about which the fathers will build their discussions. This, of course, is no more than a possibility: the code of Canon Law says nothing about it, neither mentioning it nor forbidding it, and, in the final analysis, the decision on it rests in the hands of the Pope.

6. FROM THE ANNOUNCEMENT OF THE COUNCIL TO THE CONVOCATION OF THE CONCILIAR FATHERS

THE WHOLE PROCESS of the organization of a council is not something which is left to chance; it is regulated both by the prescriptions of Canon Law which are relevant to it and by a kind of jurisprudence rooted in the experience the Church has gained at preceding councils. From the time that John XXIII made announcement of the coming council, attention has been focused upon the First Vatican Council, of which, it will be recalled, the predecessors of his holiness had caused a study to be made. This means that the lessons of that council will be heeded in order that the coming gathering may be carried out in the best way.

When a Pope announces that he has decided to summon a council he is not restricted to one way of doing it. In June, 1867, Pius IX chose to do it solemnly. He took advantage of the presence in Rome of five hundred bishops who had come from all over the world to assist at the celebrations held in commemoration of the martyrdom of Saint Peter. John XXIII chose rather to do it more quietly, in what was, indeed, an almost confidential fashion, when he spoke in January, 1959. But from the moment in which the pontifical purpose becomes public knowledge a vast machine is set in motion, and the preparation for the council begins.

Between the announcement and the coming together of the fathers quite a time may go by. In the past, serious difficulties have sometimes presented obstacles to the carrying-out of the plan. The council known to us as that of Trent was actually convoked on three occasions. The first was in 1537, when it was set for Mantua, and later for Vicenza; but the only result was to bring to light numerous intrigues. A second convocation, in 1542, which had Trent in mind, came just prior to the declaration of war between François I of France and Emperor Charles V, and this made the meeting impossible. Finally, the third time, in 1545, success was attained, despite the military activities which had been undertaken against the Protestant League of Smalkalde. In our time such checks seem less likely, although it is difficult to imagine an ecumenical council taking place during a world war. In the case of the First Council of the Vatican, the period of delay was less than that which had marked its immediate predecessor. Announced in June, 1867, it was convoked, by the bull, *Aeterni Patris* on June 29, 1868, and it met for the first time on the feast of the Immaculate Conception, December 8, 1869. Thus, in this case, the period of preparation was more than two years long.

The reason for this is that such preparation is difficult and must be meticulous. Some of the matters which must be taken into account refer to the material conditions under which the fathers of the council are to come together, the personnel which will accompany them, the theologians and the canonists who will work with them, to say nothing of the matter of providing all kinds of necessities for all these people. Throughout history there have been councils which were so badly prepared, in terms of their material organization, that many difficulties arose. Serious food shortages marked the councils held at Lyon, while at the Council of Constance (1414-1418) the great influx of fathers and their attendants into that small city, to say nothing of the numerous clerics who had flocked to the place, caused a crisis in living costs, and rent and food costs rose tenfold. At Trent, even though the attendants were fewer in number, they were enough to overcrowd a town which was really no more than a straggling village of six thousand in normal population. The consultors of the commissions did not even have an office in which to work, and many canonical texts of the utmost importance were composed at the side of a bed or scribbled on the writer's knees for a desk. And it sometimes happened that the coming together of men from the four quarters of the globe posed health problems. Thus, the Council of Trent had to be moved to Bologna for a time in the spring of 1547 in order to avoid the epidemic of typhus which the imperial troops brought in their wake. And so it was that in the capital of the Province of Emilia there was perfected the Tridentine doctrine of the sacraments. Of course, when the council meets in a great capital like Rome, these situations are not likely to arise, even though the problem of providing lodgings for so many visitors is not always an easy one.

I need not say that the intellectual preparation is even more important than is the material organization of the council. The plans made for the First Council of the Vatican were infinitely superior to those which served at Trent, where far too much was left to be improvised; and it can fittingly serve as a model. When Pius IX had announced that the council was to be held, he asked all the cardinals resident in Rome to make suggestions to him. These reports were then studied by a commission of five cardinals who set up a first draft of a program. A certain number of bishops and of scholars of Catholic universities were then consulted about this program, and five committees were appointed to work on the preparation of the schedules about which the fathers would debate. This, by and large, is the method to be used in our time, but even further refined.

From the time the council was officially announced—actually, when the communiqué from the press office of the Vatican was published—there began the phase we may call antepreparatory. The Pope and those associated with him made an initial suggestion concerning the broad outline of the chief questions which might come before the council. At the same time, an extensive consultation of the bishops of the whole world was undertaken, each one being invited to state the problems that to him seemed most important and most pressing. At the same time, the Pope set about selecting men capable of guiding the preparatory work, which means drawing up the schedules (*schema* in Greek; plural: *schemata*) destined to serve as the basis of the conciliar discussions. A certain number of commissions or committees have also been constituted in this way. Each has at its head the cardinal who, as prefect or secretary, directs the Roman Congregation (that is to say, the ministry)* which deals with corresponding matters, and each has attached to it a secretary specially chosen from among the most accomplished of the specialists concerned with the matter with which the commission will have to deal, as well as members chosen from different countries, and editorial assistants or *minutanti*. Once these commissions are set up, the antepreparatory phase is considered closed, and the actual preparation begins.

This is essentially given up to the work of the commissions. By scrutinizing the reports which have been sent in by the bishops, the members of the commissions are enabled to set up the list of questions which are to be put before the Church and to analyze the suggested solutions, setting the results of this great inquiry in the framework of Canon Law and the data of tradition. It must be emphasized that this work is done in-

---

* The one exception is Archbishop Martin J. O'Connor, who does not direct a Roman Congregation, but is President of the Pontifical Commission for Motion Pictures, Radio and Television.

dependently of the Roman Curia, and even though some members of the committees may be men concerned with administrative matters at the Vatican, the conciliar committees are distinct from the dicasteries; they do not function in the same way nor on the same plane.

Once the schedules have been prepared they must be submitted to the Pope. For the purpose of examining them a *central commission* has been set up, and of this committee it is the Sovereign Pontiff himself who is chairman. He actually makes the final decision as to which schedules shall be presented to the Council; he it is who determines the form in which this shall be done. It is understood, of course, that bishops have the right to propose new questions for discussion even after the opening of the council; but the Pope reserves to himself the right either to admit these or to rule them out of order. At the same time rules of procedure are set forth in order that discussion may be confined within suitable limits in order to avoid the sort of filibustering which might go on forever and lead nowhere. In order to rectify the propensity exhibited at Trent for endless discussion a set of regulations was prepared for the First Council of the Vatican which was discovered to be so exceedingly rigorous that it was necessary to modify it.

A tremendous attention is given to details in this preparation: this is for the reason that the more complete is this preparation the more effective and the better ordered will the council be. History assures us how great was the error which, in the case of Trent, granted to the council itself the setting-up of its own program and making regulations about its own deliberations. When it is judged that preparation has been sufficiently made, the next step is to proceed to the actual convocation. A papal bull, named, as an encyclical, from its introductory words, gives the year and the place of the meeting. Each one of the fathers receives a brief calling upon him to attend to attend. Nothing is left for those called to sit in these solemn sessions of the Church but to set forth on their journey with the secretaries whom they have chosen to accompany them.

7. THE COUNCIL GOES INTO SESSION

ONCE THE COUNCIL has met, work begins. I need not say that not all the members of the assembly undertake their labors simultaneously: one can scarcely imagine a thousand men debating, for months, on a medley of problems. The result of such a state of affairs would certainly be slight. At the First Vatican Council the schedules were distributed among the fathers who examined with the aid of their own advisors and then drew up their own comments in writing. A committee of twenty-four of the conciliar fathers was then set up for the purpose of preparing the texts of proposed decrees, some of them being entirely re-written. Then this new version of the formularies was submitted to the fathers so that they might again express their reactions to them. After the text had been agreed upon, it was presented to the general sitting— called also the general congregation—where all the fathers might exercise their right to join in the general discussion. This is a right of which they were not deprived: it may be recalled that on the question of the Primacy of the Pope and his infallibility, it was necessary that, during fourteen general sessions, there be heard seventy-four speakers out of one hunderd and thirty.

Discussion has to be free. No object is to be set aside before being examined. No difficulty is to be willingly passed over. At the Council of Florence it took seven months of debating to explore the divergencies between the Eastern and Western Churches. At the Council of Trent six months were required to allow the fathers to come to an agreement on the question of justification. Each father, being convinced that in him resides a portion of the universal *magisterium* or teaching authority, feels that the government of the Church is upon his shoulders, and he can do no less than defend to the last ditch what he believes to be the truth. And it has often happened, as the history of the councils testifies, that truth has been defended with a boldness which brooked no attention to prudence or human respect. So it was that, upon his arrival at the Council of Trent where the fathers had begun to chatter of reform as if it meant only the reformation of others, the Archbishop of Braga, Bathélemy des Martyrs, cried out: "It seems to me that it is the most eminent lords themselves who first of all are in need of the greatest reform!" But, of course, he was regarded as being a saint.

In a practical sense, freedom of discussion and the progress of the work are things which depend on the ability, the largeness of spirit, and the authority of the dignitaries who act as chairmen of the committees and general sessions. The presidency of the council is something which is vested in the sovereign Pontiff, although he exercises it through legates. Therefore, the climate of the council depends, to a large degree, on the manner in which the instructions of the Pope are carried out by his legates. At the First Vatican Council there was, at times, an impression felt that some of the Chairmen were going even beyond the wishes of Pius IX; and, often enough, discussions were interrupted although they might have led to useful results. As an example, it may be recalled that when Bishop Strossmayer asked that a somewhat inexact phrase in the decree of faith, which ascribed rationalistic atheism to Luther and Calvin, be eliminated to avoid the risk of making wider the breach which divided Catholic from separated brethren, the presiding chairman absolutely opposed the motion of amendment. Similarly, an American, Bishop Verot of Savannah, was told to be quiet, when, during a discussion of

the duties of ecclesiastics, he suggested that it would be oppor-
tune to revise the breviary in order to eliminate from it some
of the more romantic and less credible tales which the lessons
contain. He was thinking, especially, of such as the legend,
supposedly founded on the authority of Saint Augustine,
which tells us that the paralytic at the pool of Bezetha had
spent thirty-eight years on its edge before being healed by
Christ. The chairman accused Verot of being wanting in respect for the Fathers of the Church.

But, under the presidency of larger-minded chairmen, of
men who were at the same time capable and firm, discussion
could be more lively, for theology, unlike music, does not always soothe the savage breast. At Trent more than a few in-
cidents verged on the truculent. One day when one of the
Spanish bishops was asserting his opinion with a little too much
"bounce" one of the other fathers called out: "Do you think
we are holding this Council in Toledo?" The doctrinal orthodoxy of the French was held in suspicion by some, but they replied spiritedly to their critics. One of the French bishops,
when speaking about the necessary reform of the Curia, was
interrupted by the ironic gibe: "Listen to the cock; how well
he crows." The Frenchman wittily replied: "Yes, indeed;
and remember that it was at the crowing of the cock that Saint
Peter repented and wept!" How discreet was this allusion to
certain denials of Christian behaviors. And, sometimes these
disagreements were more than verbal. The bishops of south
Italy and the orientals found themselves in opposition to each
other on the question of justification, and, as their anger
mounted, one of the Italians, Bishop Sanfelice of Cava, seized
the beard of Bishop Zanettino with such an excess of energy
that half of the hairy ornament came off in his hand. For this
he was expelled from the council.

At the First Council of the Vatican things did not quite
reach this stage although the Bishop Foulon of Nancy did

write to one of his correspondents, "Many of the speakers seemed to me to be talking with cocked revolvers in their hands."

We ought not be astonished at these side shows in what was a great event; for, although supernatural in its nature and in its aim, the council does not cease to be an assembly made up of men, and like any such gathering, it has its parties, or leanings, in one direction or another. The same bishop of Nancy said, "We have our right and our left." There were all kinds of currents, plots, and intrigues. The thing to be remembered is that these human elements did no real violence to the will to serve the glory of God and of the Church which animated the entire assembly.

Pius IX once said, with the good-humor characteristic of him: "There are always three movements in a council: that of the devil who tries to upset everything; that of man who seeks to confuse; and that of the Holy Spirit who clears all things up . . ."

Actually, the experience of past councils shows that after the storm of discussion has died down and when the time has come for the vote to be taken, the fathers show concern only for the major interests of the Church and that they really vote as their consciences dictate. Moreover, every vote constitutes a public statement because, just as in the conclave for the election of a Pope, each must be signed; the ballots are not secret. In the council, furthermore, neither the voters themselves nor the tellers are bound by the obligation to secrecy which obtains at the conclave. Each man stands behind his action.

Finally, when all the parts of a schedule have been voted upon in the sessions, a solemn meeting is held, at which the Pope himself personally presides. As I have already pointed out, this session has a character entirely liturgical and is like those at which canonizations are pronounced or dogmas are proclaimed. From this time forward, the decisions of the council acquire the force of law in the Church, provided of course, as Canon 227 requires, the Pope confirms the decrees. This is an indispensable condition, indeed, of their validity.

8. "CONSENSI ET SUBSCRIPSI": "I HAVE AGREED AND SIGNED"

A QUESTION remains concerning the manner of voting in the council. It might seem that here we are dealing with a simple point of procedure; but, as a matter of fact, we face something that pierces to the very heart of the matter, touching on the essential distinction which differentiates a council from a lay assembly. It is well known that in any gathering there are two means of attaining a result: it may be apparent that all minds are in agreement upon a decision which has been considered, or, otherwise, by means of the computation of votes, a majority—whether it be simple, or of two-thirds, or of three-quarters—is shown to be in favor of one side of a question or another. It is this second method which obtains in parliaments and in similar institutions; but a council is not an assembly of this sort. For this very reason the principle of unanimity is that on which decisions are based.

The matter must be rightly understood. As a practical measure, in both the committee meetings and in the general sessions, votes are taken, and it is by a majority—a simple majority—that a text is either accepted or rejected. However, there is no basis, either in Canon Law or in tradition, that would justify the idea that an absolute majority of votes is necessary or even determining. The majority vote is actually no more than a guiding post. It serves to make clear, for the majority, the real thought of the Church upon a point or upon a rule of action which, on the whole, it would consider necessary. Those who do not vote in the sense of the majority may be considered as having been unaware of this opinion of the Church, or as having misunderstood it; but from the time it reaches the formed staged, they then adhere to it. Unanimity is, therefore, *a posteriori*, but it encompasses all the voters exactly as though they had voted in the sense of the final decision. This is, indeed, the meaning of the formulary in which all the fathers sign the decrees of the council: *consensi et subscripsi*, which is to say, "I make myself one with, I adhere to, the consensus; I join in the unanimous sense of my brethren."

It is in line with this perspective that the events which marked the end of the First Vatican Council are to be understood. When a first vote indicated that Papal Infallibility would certainly be agreed to by the great majority of the Assembly, those who were opposed * to it took counsel together and, at the suggestion of four among them, Cardinal Mathieu, Bishop Darboy, Bishop Dunpanloup, and Bishop Strossmayer, sixty-one decided to retire from the council; fifty-five wrote a joint letter to the Pope; and six others wrote to him individually in order to explain their positions. So it was that, on July 18, 1870, of the 535 Conciliar Fathers who were present, there were but two who voted *non placet*. These were Bishop Riccio of Cayazzo (near Naples), and Bishop Fitzgerald, who then held the see of Little Rock, Arkansas. But, at the time the result was proclaimed both Bishop Riccio and Bishop Fitzgerald declared that they adhered to it. Later, one by one, all those who had absented themselves submitted, although some of them, like Bishop Strossmayer and Cardinals Rauscher and Von Schwartzenberg, took a long time for reflection.

The method of procedure, which does honor to the Church, cannot be understood except it be considered in reference to the spiritual data which form the basis of the council, the lessons learned from the Scriptures and from tradition. The

---

* The opposition, for the most part, was in respect to the opportuneness of the definition, rather than to the doctrine itself.

Acts of the Apostles actually states that at the protocouncil which had assembled at Jerusalem in 49-50, the decision was one taken in unanimous concord. Pius IX did not wish to say anything other than this when, in his prologue to the decree on faith, he proclaimed: "We, the bishops of the whole world, meeting and judging together, united in the Holy Spirit in the council . . ." Nor does John XXIII have any other desire when he writes: "We pray that the council may reopen all eyes to the sight of the Apostles united at Jerusalem after the Ascension of Jesus into heaven, in oneness of thought and of prayer with Peter as they are gathered about Peter . . ."

Once again, it must be said, it is the Pauline conception of the Church as the Mystical Body which makes comprehensible the meaning and the extent of an attitude otherwise singular; for even though the members are able to think otherwise than does the visible head of the church, once the head has made the decision, then the whole body strives to carry it out.

Moreover, it is on this self-same conception that the infallibility of the council rests. This infallibility is an article of faith. It is a consequence of the promise made by Christ when He said that He is present in the Church, that He will protect it from error. Saint Athansius was thinking of this guarantee when he applied to the Nicene Creed an expression which seems surprising: "This is the Lord's own word." So was it also when Saint Gregory Magnus declared that he honored the decisions of the first four ecumenical councils as he honored the *Four Gospels*. Up until the time of the Reformation, belief in the infallibility of the councils was constant and universal; it is only since the conciliar crisis in which evident excess had been committed that the more "papal" of theologians considered it a matter for discussion.

What is this status of this infallibility by the side of the Papal Infallibility which was proclaimed at the First Council of the Vatican? It is clear that they do not contradict each other. If the episcopal college truly possesses fullness of power, it is in union with its head, in close communion with him. But Papal Infallibility can never be opposed to that of the council because, contrary to what some may think, it cannot be opposed to that of the Church. It is enough to re-read the text of the decree which proclaims Papal Infallibility to be certain of this. "The Roman Pontiff, possesses, by reason of the divine assistance, when he speaks *ex cathedra*, that infallibility *with which the Divine Redeemer has willed to enrich his Church*." One may well underline the final words: They serve to answer the criticisms urged against the dogma of Papal Infallibility by those, be they Eastern Orthodox or Protestant, who think of the Pope as being able, at will, to invent dogmas and to impose their acceptance on the community of believers. The Pope is infallible because he is the head of the Church and because he speaks in the name of the Church and for the Church. It is certain that his infallibility is personal, that is to say, that in order to exercise it the formally expressed consent of the Church is not required. Nonetheless, he exercises it in conformity with tradition and the universal consensus. Have we not seen, as a matter of fact, that Pius IX consulted the episcopate of the entire world before he promulgated the doctrine of the Immaculate Conception, and did not Pius XII do the same before defining that of the Assumption of the Holy Virgin?

The stipulation of Canon Law that the decrees of the Council must be ratified by the Pope to be valid also indicates the total union of this double authority within the Church, an authority which flows from the primacy of the Pope and an authority which proceeds from the whole body of the episcopate. As we have seen, it is summed up in the formulary by which signatures are placed at the foot of the conciliar decrees: *consensi et subscripsi*.

9. THE ACTA OF THE COUNCIL

ONCE THE text of a decree has been duly established, voted upon, and approved by the Pope, and then solemnly proclaimed, there remains one further thing to be done: the faithful must be made aware of it, must be *published*, in the technical sense of that term.

It is well known that, at the present time, every pontifical document is considered to have legal force three months after it appears in the *Acta Apostolicae Sedis*, an organ of the Vatican which has this publication as its principal function. This has been so, however, for but a relatively short time, because it was only in 1908 that Pius X made use of the idea conceived by a priest, Pietro Avanzini who, privately and unofficially, had established the *Acta Sanctae Sedis*. The Pontiff decided to found an *official journal* for the Church. Formerly, encyclicals had been simply sent to the bishops and to the great universities who then communicated them to the faithful. This method of circulation gave rise to constant discussions about the authenticity of the text. Publication in an official journal has infinitely improved the situation.

Do the *Acta* and decrees of a council fall within the scope of this journal? There is no historical precedent to which we can appeal, inasmuch as there has been no council since 1908. But it is evident that their publication ought be safeguarded in some analogous fashion. The *Acta* of Trent were brought out in an official form in 1564, and the *Acta* of the First Vatican Council, published by the semi-official daily newspaper of the Holy See, *Osservatore Romano*, were later issued as an official publication. From the time of its announcement the Second Vatican Council has benefited by numerous and most careful official publications concerning it. As early as the beginning of November, 1960, there appeared the first volume inaugurating a series of *Acta et Documenta Concilio Oecumenico Vaticano Apparando,* and its continuation has been promised. The printing of the text—in Latin, be it understood —is restricted to the official press of the Vatican, the famous *Typographia polyglotta,* which owes its foundation to Sixtus V and Gregory XIII, and its admirable organization to Gregory XV, in 1622.

From what I have said no one ought infer that the *Acta* of the councils anterior to Trent are lost or forgotten. As Bishop Jedin has written: "There is no field of religious history, not even that of hagiography, which is based upon better or more complete sources than the history of the councils." The proof of this is to be seen in the enormous interest which has been devoted to these church assemblies; theologians and canonists alike have given themselves to their study. At the commencement of the sixteenth century, when the printer's art was but fifty years old, a learned Frenchman, Jacques Merlin, set himself to building up a collection of conciliar *Acta* and decrees. He soon had many successors, who more or less repeated the work he had done, with a view to making it more extensive and more complete. Among them were Pierre Crabbé, a Belgian Franciscan, who was followed by the Carthusian, Surius, and then by Canon Bini. Powerful personages helped in these enterprises: Pope Sixtus V and Paul V, who, by the patronage they gave to a Roman edition, lent to it a character at least semiofficial; Cardinal de Richelieu, who took a personal interest in the Louvre edition, an admirable collection of thirty-seven folio volumes. Since those days there has been continuing progress in the work of establishing the best texts and in perfecting the historical commentaries. The edition of Paul V presented the Greek texts of the Eastern Councils, for the first time, and this example was not lost. The great collections made by the French Jesuits Labbe and

Coquart, (and afterwards, by the Jesuit Hardouin,) were each authoritative in turn until the second half of the eighteenth century when the learned Florentine cleric, Giovanni-Domenico Mansi, a member of the Congregation of the Mother of God, began a monumental compilation, the *Amplissima collectio* in thirty-one enormous volumes which, revised and completed down to our own times has not ceased to serve as a basis for all studies in conciliar history. The last edition in French of this work, edited at Lyon between 1899 and 1927 by J. B. Martin and L. Petit, numbers no less than fifty volumes. The edition made by the Monks of Maria-Laach and published at Freiburg-im-Breisgau, is the only one that differs substantially from that of Mansi.

It is a curious thing that these great collections were not restricted to the publication of the *Acta* of the ecumenical councils: they even included the decrees of some national councils and synods, and even of some provincial assemblies. At times it is easy to see that there was a special bias in the choice of these lesser assemblies. (Such was the case with the Jesuit Hardouin who, suspected of a leaning to Gallicanism, became involved in serious difficulties with the Roman authorities.) More often, it was simply the desire for wider knowledge which suggested this procedure to these editors, and by this inclusiveness they hoped to show how the ecumenical councils, although they marked decisive stages in the life of the Church, were closely knit to the serious and unceasing effort which has been constantly made to "ransom the time" by applying to each age the lessons to be gained from the divine Gospel.

In addition to the official publication of the conciliar *Acta*, account must be taken of the presentation of documents by historians who wish to present a council in its proper political and social climate, to estimate the reaction which it has aroused, and to measure the influence which its decisions have had. Therefore in order to understand the official edition of the *Acta* of Trent, one must necessarily turn also to the very careful work still being pursued by the learned Germans of the Gorres Society in their famous twelve volumes devoted to the *Concilium Tridentinum*, or to the volumes of the Roman periodical which is wholly devoted to this famous six-teenth century assembly. It is by these means that one may realize what was done by the committees and the meetings which gave to the Church (an impulse to) so brilliant a renewal.

10. "MANIFESTING" OF THE CHURCH

THOUGH WE have unveiled the principles upon which the council is based, the rules governing its composition, the scheme of its working, and even have reckoned all that the Church owes to it in the domain of dogma and discipline, we have not said all there is to say about the institution. History tells us that an ecumenical council is more than a gathering of prelates who meet to discuss and issue documents of which, generally speaking, only specialists are explicitly aware. Were it no more than an academy of theology or Canon Law, the occurrence of an ecumenical council would not be what it has been every time, during the course of the centuries, it has taken place—an event of major significance.

We are faced with something of great historical importance, and hence I must emphasize the significance of what has been in process ever since the time when, in the Roman monastery of Saint Paul's-Without-the-Walls, the announcement of a new council was made known on January 25, 1959.

Theoretically, this is merely a Church matter; as a matter of fact, the whole world has expressed compelling interest in this ecclesiastical meeting. Without reverting to the ecumenical

councils of the East which, many times, offer to popular interest no more than the spectacle of theological quarrels, the
general councils of medieval Christianity always stirred up
currents of opinion and often attracted enormous crowds.
The council of 1215, meeting about Innocent III at the
Lateran, drew to Rome more than three thousand clerics and
so many sightseers that the Basilica of Saint John Lateran was
not big enough to accommodate the throng which pressed into
the district whenever the solemn sessions were held. The
Council of Florence (1438-1445) attracted to the city of the
red lily great crowds of Western and Eastern Christians filled
with concern for what it would mean in respect to the relationship between the two Churches, and this was a subject of
discussion outside the council itself and as far away as Paris
and Constantinople. The mere announcement of the Council
of Trent aroused currents of opinion that often reached violence, some people approving of it, others being seriously disturbed. It aroused political reactions, notably among followers of Luther and in the Church of England. The varied
episodes which marked the council's course echoed in government chanceries, and its conclusions even upset some of the
temporal powers. So it was with all the councils which were
held during the time that the West thought of itself as Christian and when the Church was a force to be reckoned with.
Even the First Vatican Council, in mid-nineteenth century
days, when the world was already on the way to being de-
Christianized, made a considerable stir. It was a matter of concern to the civil governments, and prime ministers spoke of it
before their legislative bodies; the press reported on it with
great care to readers, and from its opening sent correspondents
to Rome. The Eternal City was literally invaded by Catholics
from all over, among whom women were by no means the
least heated in discussions about the case of Pope Honorius

and the validity of the decrees of Constance. Veuillot called them the "gossipers" of the council, while Pasquin satirically termed them "matriarchs." It was more than mere curiosity which lay beneath all this.

If an ecumenical council arouses this kind of attention, it is because by coming together at a time of grave crisis in the life of the Church, it serves notice that the Church is about to take a definite stand. That Church, which sometimes seems to overlook what is happening for a long time, then vigorously asserts itself. At Trent it replied to the attack of Protestant variation, just when it appeared that it had resigned itself to seeing the revolt make great strides. At the First Vatican Council it affirmed with striking forcefulness its union with the great Pope who had resolved to stand out in opposition to the tendencies of the modern world, to rationalism, and to laicism. This important character of the universal assembly is noted in the prologue to the constitution on Catholic faith decreed by the Vatican council; all that is set forth therein is expressed with great depth and unusual strength by reason of the solemn nature of its utterance. In the most exact sense of the word, the council is a manifesting of the Church, a kind of epiphany.

This manifesting can have more than one meaning. Every one of the great councils of the Church has had its own special kind of attraction, its own background. It is in a given time, in definite historical circumstances, that a council meets, and if the Church is not *of* the world, it is *in* the world: what is done in the world is reflected in the discussions held in the assembly of the Church. Trent was essentially a battle-ground, and if its work flowed far beyond the frame-work of a mere defense or counter attack—contrary to what is implied in that very debatable term, the "counter-reformation"—it is nonetheless true that, in their labors, the fathers never allowed themselves to lose sight of the criticisms of their adversaries. The First Council of the Vatican was assuredly colored by the situation in which the papacy then found itself and by the increasingly menacing forces by which it had been surrounded for more than thirty years.

The circumstances, the characteristic notes of the age are not, however, by any means the only elements which lend to a council its own peculiar aspect; the actions of the Pope who convokes it can be of prime significance; by the way in which he directs its work he can make of *his* council an occasion to exhibit and enhance the prestige of the Holy See; he can fashion it into a weapon in the warfare which is life; he can make it an organ of internal reform. From the moment the Second Vatican Council was announced, everyone could know, in knowing him who has called it, what its climate will be.

As a public manifesting of the Church the council cannot fail to bring the Church into public notice, demonstrating that it exists, that it works, that it counts for something. Something then occurs which, however visible it may be to him who knows what to look for, is of an internal nature. Every ecumenical council affords to the Church the opportunity to renew itself. The coming together of so many men in the light of the Holy Spirit, their common striving the better to know the will of God and the higher interests of the Church, result in freeing consciences and institutions of that hard shell of routine which passing years have bound around them. New problems are noted; new solutions come into view. It was from the Council of Trent that the modern Church emerged, that Church of a century of great souls which has endured into our own time. It was at the First Council of the Vatican that there was affirmed the wondrous nature and the practical force of the papacy, which has become in our own day increasingly authoritative.

Canon Law, it should be recalled, points out that the council is no more than an aspect "of the Church's life" which is as much as to say that, in principle, it is not something essential to it. But therein, precisely, does its importance lie: it shows to the world that the Church is a living force.

III

The Outlook for the
Second Vatican Council

———— ◀◆▶ ————

1. TWO YEARS PASS: THE "VIGIL
OF PENTECOST"

THE FIRST of the three stages which may be noted in the
history of any council has already reached its end so far as the
Second Vatican Council is concerned, and the second stage is
vigorously under way. By autumn of 1960, the "antepreparatory" phase had come to a close after preliminary planning of
the main questions to be studied, after a general consultation
with all those who are entitled to take seats in the assembly,
and, finally, with the selection of the men who would be asked
to prepare the work of the council. One might mark the beginning of the second phase as dating from the audience given
by the Pope on November 14, 1960, to the members of the
various committees who were preparing to begin their work.
At this time he explained to them what he conceived the role of
the coming council to be.

But, what is of greater import than these results in the practical order, which are of interest mainly to specialists, is that
the council, even before it has begun, may be said to have al-

ready fulfilled a large part of its task. One of the attributes—and by no means the least—of an ecumenical council is that it is a "manifestation" or an "epiphany" of the Church, in the root sense of the word. Thus, it must be granted, after a glance at public opinion, that this end has been attained. Two days after the announcement at Saint Paul's, the Archbishop of Milan, Cardinal Montini, said that the council would be "an historical event of the first order, the greatest that has ever been, and something of interest to the entire world." But it was not only princes of the Roman Church who spoke in such terms. Prominent religious leaders, not of the Catholic communion, men who owed varied allegiances, emphasized the importance of holding a council. "This council will be a prime event in itself," said Dr. Marc Boegner, president of the Protestant Federation of France, when he addressed the Central Committee of the World Council of Churches. Eastern Orthodox theologians, like Patriarch Athenagoras of Constantinople, and Charles Malik, who had been president of the Assembly of the United Nations, expressed themselves in similar terms. The Archbishop of Canterbury, Dr. Geoffrey Francis Fisher, primate of the Church of England, has shown by word and deed what his thoughts are, as when he visited the Pope. The press of the whole world has shown how great is its interest in this event: there is not a single journal, nor any one of the great reviews, nor even one radio commentator, who has failed to discuss the papal decision. And this is true even of Soviet Russia, where attacks have the effect of praise.

However, a number of considerations emphasize the fact that the council is not simply a manifestation of the Church to the world. As well as affording external testimony of the Church's vital force, the council must also, and indeed already is so doing, give interior manifestation of this vitality. An ecumenical council, it is to be recalled, always means a renewal of force. The Second Vatican Council will be no exception to the rule: there are already numerous signs foreshadowing this. The very way in which it was announced and the methods which have marked its preparation have been enough to indicate, very directly, that a will for renewal is guiding its work. In the Roman circles particularly responsible for getting this great enterprise under way, this willingness displays itself by the alacrity, at once cheerful and serious, and by the contagious enthusiasm with which preparations are being made. "A kind of jolt is now shaking the Church, freeing the boldest thought and turning ingrained habits upside down," is how the situation has been put by a well-informed journalist. This will for renewal is in the forefront of Catholic opinion. The council is certainly the focus of consuming curiosity: it is most eagerly awaited.

Substantially, the thought of Catholics was perfectly expressed by the rector of the Roman Church of Saint-Louis-des-Français, Bishop Baron, when he wrote: "The essential youthfulness of the Church must reveal itself in its outward appearance, for the by-wash of history has inevitably covered it with the garments of time, garments which become, in time, things of shreds and patches." Believers, searchers after belief, even the unbelieving, are penetrated by the feeling that great things are possible; moreover, that they are probable. The mass of men are turning to face the teaching Church and their minds are full of questions.

Can it be that it is all right to say that replies to these questions are already in formation?

"The announcement of the council," writes Father Marlé, "has reawakened marvelously in the minds of great bodies of Christians the decision to share, both for personal and altruistic ends, in the advancement of the work of the Universal Church, which has in view the well-being and benefit of the whole Christian world. It is true that the dogma of the Communion of Saints has never been entirely lost sight of in our Church. But it is only when it is concretely practiced that it is most profoundly understood. To the exclusivist notion of a treasury of grace in which one shares there then is added the compelling impulsion of a common work to be undertaken."

The Holy Father, by drawing attention in his very first declaration to his children to the dramatic disunity which sunders Christians, has directed his Catholic sons to turn toward the problems of "others" that they may feel that this problem is not a marginal one, beyond their scope, but lies rather at the very core of their own concern. "The council will be pointed toward the 'others'—our separated brethren," as Father Congar has said. In a sense, this is already so.

Without any doubt, great possibilities are here. New opportunities are open to the Church of Christ simply because Christ's vicar has called upon it to face its problems. We have not come to that "Pentecost" of which Pope John XXIII has spoken; but we are keeping its vigil. How fine a thing it is that, already, from the hearts of millions of Christians there well up those words which are appropriated to the act of offering in the Mass of the Vigil of Pentecost: "Send forth Thy Spirit, O Lord, and all shall be re-made; the face of the earth will be renewed."

2. VATICAN II

ON THE covers of the cardboard binders in which they assemble their papers and notes, the members of the preparatory committees can read the printed words: *Vatican II*. The same formulary is used on the cover of the volume of *Acta* of the council—the first of the pro-preparatory series —which has already been printed. Strictly speaking, there are two ways in which it can be taken: it might mean the second part of the Vatican Council inasmuch as the first council remains prorogued, *sine die,* and is not yet closed. Or it may, and perhaps should, be taken to mean the Second Vatican Council. It seems certain that it is the second interpretation which will prevail, although we do not yet know whether the Pope will pronounce officially the end of the First Vatican Council when he convokes that which is now to follow. History will then record the Second Vatican as succeeding the First Vatican, just as it has marked two councils of Nicea, four of Constantinople, two of Lyon, and five of the Lateran.

None of the halls of the Vatican palace is suitable to accommodate, with fitting dignity, the number of fathers and their secretarial staffs which will be present at this council. It seems, therefore, likely that the nave of Saint Peter's Basilica will be set aside for the assembly. At the First Council of the Vatican, they used the right arm of the transept, "the nave of Saints Processis and Martinian" which, by the judicious use of partitions and curtains under the direction of the architect Vespignani had been transformed into a hall 150 feet in length by sixty-six in width, with platforms around the sides. There were, however, serious acoustical problems, which were only imperfectly solved in an age to which the use of the loud speaker to amplify voices was unknown.

Of one thing we may now be fairly certain, and that is the list of those who will be summoned to the council. If the presently existing principles of Canon Law are observed, the voting members of the council will be the cardinals, archbishops, residential bishops, superiors of religious orders, prelates and abbots *nullius.* Titular bishops, nuncios, vicars and prefects apostolic, and certain theologians and canonists will enjoy only debating rights. This arrangement remained unchanged by the Pope in the Bull of Convocation of December 25, 1961. Careful calculation has established that 2,816 will be summoned, of whom 1,898 are in the first category, and 918 are in the second. This will be three times as many as were summoned to be fathers of the First Council of the Vatican. Modern means of transportation will make the journey to Rome much easier than it was one hundred years ago, and there will, doubtless, be only a few absentees.

The division of the fathers among the varied nations furnishes us with an interesting indication of the truly international and ecumenical character of this assembly. There will be 313 Italian prelates, while the rest of Europe—Russia not being counted—will furnish 415 representatives. South America will send 401, and North America 196. It is a curious and arresting fact that all of Europe, which represents 47% of world Catholicism, will have only a 38% representation in the assembly. The two Americas, which number 43% of the Catholics in the world, will have, in the council, no more than a representation of 31.5% of the fathers. By contrast, Asia, Africa, and Oceania—the whole of the "third World"—which numbers only 10% of world Catholicism, will have 20.5% of the council membership.

As far as the laity are concerned, it is known that, in the canonical sense, they have no claim to open participation in the work of the assembly. According to law, the Second Vatican Council will be a meeting of the bishops, a council of the teaching Church. However, there is to be detected a tendency to associate with it, at least indirectly, the Church taught. Many bishops, prior to turning in the reports which they had been requested to send, consulted the heads of Catholic action movements; for, when it is a question of determining what pastoral problems exist, it is well to go to the members of the flock in whose interest the pastoral care of the bishop is exercised. Some personages in Rome who are members of the preparatory committees have indicated that "laymen who are teaching in the faculties of the sacred sciences have been directly questioned" (Monsignor Glorieux). The thought has even been expressed (by Father Spiazzi) that "considering the competence and the maturity which many laymen have shown in the fields of the theological, biblical, and liturgical studies, and the experience they have attained" it is desirable that they should be consulted and listened to. The laity may not sit in flesh and bone at the council; there may be but one of them among the members of the preparatory committees; but their influence upon the council is certain.

In the delightful conference which Archbishop Roberts, formerly of the See of Bombay, gave at the Institute of International Research in March of 1959, he forthrightly declared that the conciliar "football game" would be more interesting if, in view of the fact that all the players are bishops, "the spectators might cheer on this or that player, or even make suggestions to the umpire." And then he added, enigmatically: "Lack of time prevents me from repeating to you now some stories about Pope John XXIII which prove that he has always dreamed of being an umpire."

The orientation of the council to the laity is revealed by the early evidence that the Vatican was taking special pains to assist the press in bringing to the public exact information about the council. A secretariat was set up to fulfill this function, and the secretary of the Central Committee, Archbishop Felici, has announced that special organs of information will be established in order "to obviate the diffusion of unfounded or erroneous reports." Without being prolix or too detailed, officials responsible for the organization of the council have, to some extent, abandoned the reserve traditional in such cases. One indication is that the former Vatican Secretary of State, the late Cardinal Tardini, held press conferences in which he frankly replied to questioners. It is indeed true that the council will not have, in world opinion, the kind of hearing which it should arouse, unless the public feels that problems are set honestly before it, unless it be shown freely the means which are in view in respect to their solution, and unless the whole matter be presented as something which is not being done behind closed doors.

There is a final question to be considered, and it was raised as early as July of 1959 by the noted Latinist, Cardinal Bacci: what will be the language of the council? Latin remains the official language of the Church, and, therefore, at his press conference on October 30, 1959, Cardinal Tardini formally came out in favor of the traditional idiom, "the only tongue which all the participants share in common." But he added:

"Not too much reliance should be placed on the possibility that we shall have recourse to simultaneous translation to broadcast the discourses as they are made, through the medium of individual telephonic head-pieces. It is not easy to translate Latin in this fashion, especially a Latin which does not always possess Ciceronian purity." He closed his observations by a remark which is not lacking in characteristic Roman irony: "Latin has many advantages, perhaps not the least of them is that speeches made in it may be briefer . . ."

At the First Vatican Council, Bishop Jordany of Fréjus wrote to a friend: "Once one has lost the habit of speaking Latin, it becomes an obstacle to the manifestation of thought. The Germans, the Italians, and even the Spaniards have greater ease in it than we Frenchmen. The most pitiable are those who are most forward . . ." However, Archbishop Felici has announced that "if some experience difficulties in expressing themselves in Latin, they will be permitted, by way of exception, to express themselves in their native tongues."

3. THE COMMITTEES AT WORK

"Never in conciliar history," John XXIII has said, "has there been preliminary work on so vast a scale, or in so precise and fundamental a fashion, as in the case of the Second

Council of the Vatican." These labors are those of committees and secretariats which are *ad hoc* creations.

The document issued under the title of *Superno Dei nutu* and signed by the Pope on June 5, 1960, set into motion what Father Wenger has, in truth, termed "laboratories of theological research." They number twelve organisms in all, ten committees and two secretariats, each of which is specially assigned to handle a particular group of matters. This figure is, in itself, indicative of a will for greater breadth and depth, for there were but five committees engaged in the work preparatory to Vatican I. And, even so, this figure is not necessarily final; for rumor at Rome insists that there may be set up a particular kind of committee, one whose work will join together members of many other committees, one which will be charged with problems concerning contemporary godlessness in all its forms.

One must, moreover, add to the table of committees and secretariates, which are making preparation for the council on the plane of ideas, two other organizations which function on other levels, not necessarily of much less importance. One is the Technical and Economic Secretariat charged with the material organization of this enormous assembly. The other, the Committee on Ceremonial, under the leadership of the dean of the Sacred College, Cardinal Tisserant, upon whom falls the duty, which will be no light one, of regulating the protocol of the council and of giving to the public ceremonies that character of liturgical solemnity which is fitting.

But the very list of the committees is not without significance. Their designations cover the whole field of problems which face the Church, both in regard to her inner life and to her relationships with the world. It is enough to read the list to realize the real place which these diverse questions take in the preoccupations of the Church; and this is true even of those of which the press tends to exaggerate the importance.

The Secretariat for the Unity of Christendom is evidently that most favored by public opinion; yet it is only one of twelve committees whose work must be weighed by the council.

The actual members of the committees number 862, and this figure is not necessarily final, for it is almost certain that it will be increased. Committee members have been appointed by the pro-preparatory committee which Bishop Pericleo Felici directed, under the aegis of the secretary of state. It is Bishop Felici also who serves as secretary of the Central Committee of which the Supreme Pontiff is chairman. The names of members from among the secular clergy have been suggested by the nuncios, and, from among the religious, by the superiors of religious orders. Thus have been assembled the leading theologians and the canonists, sociologists, and missiologists who are best qualified. The selection of some is very suggestive. Thus, we see as secretary of the first committee, that of theology, Father Tromp, an eminent specialist in the theology of the Church, and among its members two French religious to whom theological speculation owes much, although they have been the butt of much criticism, Father Lubac, S.J., and Father Congar, O.P. We may be sure that it was not unintentionally that the Pope has decided to call these two outcasts to take part in the most essential kind of work for the good of the council and the Church.

The division of the membership of the committees apportioned to the various nations is not less meaningful. They come from seventy different countries and all five continents are represented. It is doubtless chiefly for practical reasons, but also perhaps by reason of competency, that Europeans outnumber the others. They constitute 71% of the membership. The Americas, especially South America, have supplied only a few committee members and consultors. There are more than 150 Italians among the members, and it is not without satisfaction that Frenchmen see seventy-four of their theologians among the members of the committees, which is to say that they have been allowed a place the double of that which an exact arithmetic would have accorded them.

Both committees and secretariats have the same structural formation: a chairman, a secretary, some thirty members, as well as consultors. Side by side with these also work *minutanti*, who are minute takers and editors, and archivists who take care of documentation. The two chief personages are the chairman and the secretary. With one exception, all the chairmen are cardinals, being the same men as those who in the dicasteries have charge of the corresponding Roman congregation. For example, Cardinal Agagianian, who directs the Congregation of the Propagation of the Faith or World Mission Society, is the chairman of the committee concerned with missions. By contrast, all the secretaries have been selected apart from the curia, and it is clear that an intentionally universal spirit has directed their choice. Among them are but three Italians and only one Frenchman. There are, however, a Ukranian, an Englishman, and a Canadian. The chairman and the secretary hold positions of importance. They can exercise considerable influence on the discussions, especially when, as is generally the case, their competence is such that they are able to come to grips with the whole body of the questions which lie before the committee. The climate of the council will depend to a large degree on the fashion in which they have prepared matters. Therefore the choice of Cardinal Bea, whose breadth of view is well-known, to head the Committee for the Unity of Christians, seems to be pregnant with high significance.

The preparatory committees and secretariates are housed in the offices of the Roman congregations, especially in those two great and obviously new palaces which close the east end of Saint Peter's Square at the beginning of the majestic *Via della Conciliazione*. Does this circumstance, and the fact that the chairmen are the same as the cardinal-prefects or the secretaries of the Roman congregations, indicate that the preparation of the council is no more than a kind of adjunct, a prolongation of the tasks which the functionaries of the curia normally discharge? Were this so, it would not have been necessary to set up these committees. John XXIII has insisted on the differentiation of their scope and their tasks: "To the ecumenical council belong its own structure and its own organization, and this must not be confused with the ordinary and characteristic functioning of the various dicasteries and congregations of the Roman curia, for that curia will pursue, even during the sessions of the council, its ordinary work, in accordance with the normal regulation of the general administration of the Church."

No iron-clad procedural regimen has been imposed on the committees. Of design, full liberty has been left to the chairmen, secretaries, and members themselves to organize their work, and to make use of methods which to them seem best suited to their purposes, allowing for differences in ends and means. The committees have the right to divide themselves into subcommittees, each one being particularly charged with the study of a special body of matters. Thus the Committee on the Apostolate of the Laity already comprises three subcommittees, respectively charged with matters concerning the social problem, with Catholic action, and with works of charity and education. Likewise, within the structure of the secretariat which is studying modern methods of the diffusion of thought, three committees are functioning, one for the press, another for the cinema, and a third for radio and television. It goes without saying that not only do the subcommittees pool the results of their labors, but also that the committees and the secretariat themselves can be called upon the collaborate, one with another, when the themes which they are studying are closely related. An example is provided by the Oriental Committee and the Secretariat on the Reunion of Christians.

In all cases and for all committees and secretariats, fundamental documentation is gleaned by the whole corpus—one which is, literally, monumental—of reports sent to Rome by the bishops and prelates consulted in 1959. More than two thousand seven hundred of these reports have reached Rome. Classified and summarized, they have been printed by the Vatican press in a series of large quarto volumes, identical in appearance to those which contain papal texts on the council. They form the pro-preparatory *Acta*. Three sets of volumes have been produced, one containing the reports of bishops and prelates, another proposals of the Roman curia, a third the matter submitted by the Catholic universities. But the word "volume" does not convey an idea of the tremendous number of documents which have been assembled. Volume two alone —that of the bishops and prelates—embodies eight huge tomes.*

It is known that this vast preparatory enterprise reaches its summit in a co-ordinating and policy-making agency which exercises a determining role. This is the Central Commission. It is composed of fifty-eight cardinals under the chairmanship of the Pope himself.† The Secretary is Archbishop Felici. It is this committee which selects from among the questions submitted by the different committees those which are actually to be submitted to the council; it establishes the agenda and the program of the assembly. And it is precisely for the reason that its conclusions orient the council in this or that direction and thus potentially involve the infallible authority of that as-

---

* Archbishop Felici could well cry out: "They have sent enough material to Rome to supply ten councils with material." It is said that about 5,000 proposals were sent in.

† The Central Commission is composed also of 5 patriarchs, 27 archbishops, 6 bishops and 4 superiors general of Religious Orders.

sembly that the Pope himself must retain control of its operations. These operations could not begin until the preparatory committees had submitted the results of their own work in the first versions of their schedules. Until all the reports of the

A TABLE SHOWING THE ORGANIZATIONAL PREPARATION
FOR THE COUNCIL

Committee or Secretariat	Chairman and country of origin	Secretary and country of origin
Theological Committee	Cardinal Ottaviani (Italy)	Father Tromp (Holland)
Committee on Bishops and the Government of Dioceses		Bishop Gawlina (Poland)
Committee for the Discipline of Clergy and People	Cardinal Ciriaci (Italy)	Father Bezutti (Italy)
Committee on Religious	Cardinal Valeri (Italy)	Father Rousseau (Canada)
Committee on the Discipline of the Sacraments	Cardinal Aloisi-Masella (Italy)	Father Bigador (Spain)
Committee on Liturgy		Father Bugnini (Italy)
Committee on Studies and Seminaries	Cardinal Pizzardo (Italy)	Father Mayer (Germany)
Committee on Oriental Churches	Cardinal A. Cicognani (Italy)	Father Welukyi (Ukraine)
Committee for the Missions	Cardinal Agagianian (Armenia)	Bishop Mathew (England)
Committee for the Lay Apostolate and Catholic Action	Cardinal Cento (Italy)	Monsignor Glorieux (France)
Committee on Ceremonial	Cardinal Tisserant (France)	Monsignor Nardone (Italy)
Secretariat for the Union of Christians	Cardinal Bea (Germany)	Monsignor Willebrands (Holland)
Secretariat for the Media of the Diffusion of Ideas	Archbishop O'Connor (U.S.A.)	Monsignor Deskur (Poland)
Technical and Economic Secretariat	Cardinal di Jorio (Italy)	Monsignor Guerri (Italy)
Central Committee	Pope John XXIII	Monsignor Felici (Italy)

committees have been studied by the Central Committee, the list of questions upon which the council will have to deliberate cannot be known, as the Central Committee must approve the proposed texts, or discuss and modify them, or limit itself to allowing them to stand without any expression of official approval. In the meanwhile, the program remains wrapped in profoundest secrecy.

Moreover, whatever be his rank, every member of a committee preparing the council must observe absolute secrecy about it. In principle, two members of different committees are not supposed to reveal to one another what they know of the work of their own groups unless there is real necessity to do so. Each took an oath on the day of his appointment; each has sworn to keep silent on these matters.

4. "SURVIVALS" AND "FORECAST"

Lacking any official publication of the precise subject matter with which the council will be concerned, is it quite impossible even to sum up questions which might be brought before it? *La Civiltá Cattolica*, a review edited by the Italian Jesuits, in its issue of April 1959, rightly rebuked the frivolity with which journalists laid before the public, on the heels of the Pope's announcement of the council, plans of reform which proved that those who had invented them had greater imagination than theological knowledge. However, although it be absurd to presume to give lessons to the Church by imposing upon her responsible governors a list of problems to study, it seems quite proper to try to understand the reasons behind the assembly now being prepared.

To do this successfully, there are three classes of information which can be drawn upon, and they, moreover, are intertwined. The first includes those afforded by the declarations, numerous and precise, of the Pope himself, for there has scarcely been a week since January, 1959, in which John XXIII has not spoken of the council. He has seized every occasion to draw the attention of the faithful to this enterprise and to make them realize all that it portends. On the other hand, by indicating on repeated occasions that in the preparation of the coming council it is his intention to benefit from the lessons of past councils, the Pope has thus recognized the role of legal historians who, as Bishop Jedin has put it, focus upon the past in order that they may cast a more assured eye upon the future. This does not mean that Vatican II will be, in any sense, a kind of repetition or even a mere prolongation of Vatican I or of Trent. As John XXIII has happily said: "The Church is not a museum, it is the old village well which gives water from one generation to another."

Nevertheless, by studying the councils of the past, and, in particular, the last two of them, it is possible to establish at once the soundness of their work, which it would be useless to call into question, and, on the other hand, the areas in which they failed, in which their work was incomplete.

Finally, and perhaps principally, the reasons behind a new council can be made clear if one tries to grasp the significance of what has been happening in the world since the end of the last council, of what it is that faces the Church today. It helps to know what the most difficult problems are and of what kind of solutions to them have been suggested and, perhaps, already tried.

This attempt to log, as it were, the chief reasons for a council being held will avoid certain errors of viewpoint, which are all too common. The first such error is to consider the coming assembly as being exclusively preoccupied solving the problems of Christian unity. This is well-known, for there are vast numbers waiting for "the council of unity." There is no doubt that at the first announcement of the council John

XXIII made it clear that one of its chief ends would be to work
for a reconciliation of separated brethren. And it is, moreover,
doubtless true that the whole question of unity is one which
arouses deep anguish of conscience. But it is also true that, in
the minds of those not perfectly attuned to true spiritual problems, the relationship between Christians is conceived of in
terms which are too political. According to such readers of
events, the reconciliation can take place in a manner analogous
to that which sees come into being a pact of alliance or
a treaty fostering economic mutuality. It must be said that such
is not the way the Church envisages the drama of disunity. In
exaggerating the importance granted to the problem of unity,
there is risk of forgetting that the council is an assembly of the
Catholic Church, that it is, as Cardinal Tardini has said, "an internal event in the Church. It has some external connections,
but it is focused on the Church, the episcopate, the clergy, and
the faithful." In his Encyclical, *Ad Petri Cathedram*, of July 3,
1959, John XXIII declared:

> The chief end of the council is to advance the development
> of the Catholic Faith, the renewal of Christian life among the
> people, the adaption of ecclesiastical discipline to contemporary
> conditions. Assuredly, this will afford a wonderful spectacle of
> truth, of unity, of charity, and we are confident that in seeing
> it those who are separated from this Apostolic See will see in it
> a warm invitation to seek and find unity.

This statement sets out with great precision the hierarchy of
the problems to be faced and the ends to be accomplished
by the council.

The council, although an internal event within the Church,
nevertheless has "external connections." The council will
have to face a question, fundamental ever since the Renaissance, that has become increasingly pressing since the French
Revolution. It is this: What should be the attitude of the

Church brought face to face with the contemporary world? It is evident that, for five centuries, the Church has been the object of attack in the field of ideas and in the field of actual life, and that the attack on the part of contemporary society becomes more and more violent. Should the Church fight back, treating the world simply as an adversary, or should it rather come to an understanding with the world by recognizing and adopting what is good in it? All during the nineteenth century this was the dominant question in the Church's history; and it faces the Church with even more imperious insistence today.

It would be an error of the first order to picture the council as a kind of war machine, a kind of "religious Atlantic Pact," as the Soviet Academy of Sciences has termed it, seeing in it another manifestation of "the anti-Communist tradition of the Vatican." To this Cardinal Tardini has replied that "being essentially something within the Church, the council is aimed against no one."

It would be equally erroneous to imagine that only the knowledge that it is faced with danger has led the Church to hold solemn sittings in order to consider the contemporary situation as a whole. Such a reading of the case would call it "the council of fear" and see in it the beginning of a complete reversal. In his Christmas message of 1960, the Pope thought it useful to reply to this by saying: "At this time, the lowly successor of Saint Peter is not tempted to fearfulness." Mankind, he added, has faced hours much more trying than our own. The certainty of God's promise in which one can be sure that His words will not pass away, and that His Church will endure forever, is enough to cast out all fear, just as the charity of Christ leaves no room for aggressiveness.

In the conference to which I have already referred, Bishop Roberts made use of the expression "council of survivals." He does this not with reference to the council now in preparation, but to a kind of "pre-conciliar state" which "by crystalizing the forces of Christian tradition, the treasure trove of Eastern thought, the actual data attained by scientists and military leaders as a result of nuclear warfare" brings together all men who still have faith in man and in spiritual values, uniting them in an effort to prevent the world from being swallowed by nothingness. It is not likely that Vatican II will embody this dream; moreover, it is even less likely that a pre-council would charge itself with such a program. Yet, in endeavoring to solve its own problems, which means making an effort to bring the everlasting Gospel of Christ closer to mankind, the Church can be certain that, in thus being faithful to its own calling, it will have been of service to humanity on this earth, it will have worked to insure its "survival."

The Church is not calling this council to attack her adversaries, nor to build up her defenses, nor even to set under way some spectacular campaign in the face of danger. But it is to be wished, and it is also highly probable that, in thus gathering together, the Church in council will take accurate cognizance of all the problems which face it as this twentieth century has entered upon its second half, and that the Church will work to find solutions which will be, all at once, in conformity with the Gospel with which it has been charged, with its own true interest, and with the common good of mankind. And these three ends are coalescent.

Gaston Berger, who, among the men of our time, has most lucidly analyzed our own age in all the contradictory claims it makes and all the confused hopes it cherishes, has suggested the notion of what he calls the "forecast." He tells us that the forecast is neither a doctrine nor a system. It means reflecting upon the future and gaining a broad vision of things in order that there may be brought forth a method of dealing with our fast-changing world. Would it be impertinent to suggest that, appropriate as is a "prospective, a forward-looking attitude" to the men of science, the economists, the sociologists, and the financiers to whom Gaston Berger speaks, it is even more so to the fathers of the coming council? Under the Spirit's guidance, it is the future of the Church to which they are to bend their thought and their effort—and to speak of the future of the Church is to speak of the future of mankind.

5. A CRISIS IN THE CHURCH OR A CRISIS IN THE WORLD?

IT IS by giving thought to the future, that is to say, by striving to estimate in the light of the present the shape of things to come, that one is able, without being presumptuous, to understand why the council is being held.

History shows that there have been two kinds of councils and that some have partaken of the nature of both. One kind is that of the doctrinal councils in which affirmation is made of the living tradition of the meaning of Christ's Gospel and the organization of His Church. The other kind is that of the reforming councils—taking the word *reforming* in its broadest sense—in which the Church takes occasion to reorganize itself, to refurbish its methodology, and, sometimes, to purify itself. It appears that Vatican II will belong rather to the second than to the first of these categories.

Does this mean that the Church of the twentieth century is in a state of crisis, that it stands in need of the same kind of a reformation as did the Church of the sixteenth century? Most assuredly this is not so. Cardinal Montini emphasized this aspect when, in inaugurating a study week organized by the University of the Sacred Heart, Milan, in September of 1960, he declared: "Unlike many another council, Vatican II will meet at a time when life in the Church is at once peaceful and fervent."

When the Council of Trent was held, the Church was in the grip of a four-fold crisis. There was moral contagion touching the lives not alone of the people but of vast numbers of the clergy, as well. There was intellectual ferment which plunged an ever-increasing body of Christians into heresy. There was a questioning of authority which struck at the Church's hierarchical structure. And, finally, as a direct consequence of the two preceding crises, there was a crisis of unity. It is enough to recall this situation to point out how it differs from that which prevails today, for perhaps never since its beginning was the Catholic Church more solidly united around its visible head. Perhaps never before did it enjoy a clerical body whose intellectual and moral training is so good. There is no real risk of heretical infiltration. There is no real risk of organizational schism. It is not a crisis of the Church which Vatican II will have to face.

The real problems before the Church at the present time are those of the society in which it is set. It is a truism to state that the world has undergone a greater change during the past century and a half than during the twenty or twenty-five preceding centuries. A double revolution is now in progress, one part of which affects ideas, and the other practical life. Moreover, the factors involved in both are tightly enmeshed in each other. The revolutionary progress in science and in technology have veritably turned upside down, in every sense, all the conditions under which human life is lived. It affects life not only in the sense that work is lessened, comfort increased, and distances lessened, but, thanks to medical advances, the accustomed rhythmic lines of population increase have been wholly modified, and, consequently, the balance between the masses of human-kind has been altered. Every one of these facts is literally revolutionary. The world is in a state of crisis, mankind is in a state of crisis, and the Church, transcendent indeed but nevertheless made up of men, is not able to ignore this crisis without condemning itself to become a victim to it.

One has, of necessity, to advert to and to accept the new conditions amidst which Providence calls one to live. Such, as has already been seen, is the conception John XXIII has of *up-to-dateness*; and this was likewise true, in his own day, of Pius IX. It is a matter, if one will, of an adaptation of the Church, of its modernization, despite the fact that such expressions arouse little satisfaction in the mind of the theologian to whom it is evident that the Church is changeless.

The world crisis brings many questions before the Church. Some of these concern the realm of ideas. It has been a long time—in any case not since the Renaissance, and perhaps even before—since there has been a rebellion like that of Lucifer, a rebellion against God and the faith. This rebellion assumes varied garbs, and the Church has to combat errors which are substantially the same but which appear in different forms. One hundred years ago what was called "liberalism"—a most equivocal term—was considered to be the chief enemy of dogma and the ordered structure of the Church, being thought of as the supply-sergeant of the revolution. Nowadays, when quarrels about the meaning of "liberalism" have been appeased, the Church no longer regards all liberalism as worthy of condemnation, and, in line with a true theological view, recognizes liberty to be one of the attributes of the human person and the basis of his responsibility.

But, in our day, a great many more ideologies are directed against the Church. All are essentially the same; for, whether we turn to the rationalism born of Kant, or the positivism of Auguste Comte, or the dialectical materialism of Karl Marx, or the existentialism of Sartre, we find all are rooted in what Father de Lubac has called "atheistic humanism." What is needed is a reply to the whole complex of these doctrines by opposing to them that integral humanism, the humanism of the

Incarnation, which Jacques Maritain has recognized in Christianity.

These atheistic philosophies have received impetus from the progress of the physical sciences. Although no one any longer need believe, as did Renan in his *L'Avenir de la science*, that scientific progress can guarantee to man an earthly paradise, yet there remains deeply anchored in many hearts, a certain kind of scientism which results in the denial of any revelation and in the eradication of the supernatural. Thus the value of the Biblical message, the Christian explanation of the origin of life and of man, the basis of morality, and, of course, all metaphysics appear to be in question, not so much by true savants as by those who trail after them in the fields of historical criticism, of paleontology, or of psychology. The problem of the relationship between science and faith is set before the man of the twentieth century, whether he be a Christian or not, as one of greatest urgency. What response will the Church make to this problem?

And, finally, as everyone knows, science is made manifest in technology. We are part of a world of technology, and one which, year by year, will not become less so. Now, technology brings in its train consequences which Christianity does not know how to admit. On the one hand, it results in a dehumanization of man, which shows itself openly in that degradation of man subject to the machine which Pius XI denounced in *Quadragesimo anno* as leading to the collective brutalization of the masses through ease, publicity, and other means of bringing the spirit under bondage. On the other hand, through its technical results science has exposed man of the twentieth century to risks which he will have to face. A scientist who is no professing Christian, but nevertheless, a man of conscientious sensitivity, Jean Rostand, has said: "Even beyond the complicity with which it panders to murderous passion, science is, of itself, something which we have to fear." How is the

Church to bring the Gospel of Christ into a relationship with science and technology without wholly condemning them—which would be an absurd and useless thing to do—but also without losing sight of the terrible dangers with which they surround man as a ransomed being?

On an entirely different plane, a plane wholly human, the Church sees set before her other questions which are equally serious. The industrial revolution of the nineteenth century has altered, in a decisive way, the social classes, and its effects are far from being fully worked out. The society into which the Church has sunk such deep roots, is shaking; perhaps it is ready to fall apart. Like the Roman Empire in the fourth century, it has been the victim of terrifying attacks, not of barbarian tribes on the march of conquest, but of what Ortega y Gasset terms "a vertical invasion."

Rather than give heed to those within its ranks who were quick to denounce the exploitation of man by man, the Church has gauged the importance of this problem only after some delay. The illuminating encyclical *Rerum novarum* of Leo XIII did not prevent the "great scandal" spoken of by Pius XI, the loss to the Church of the working class. All the efforts made since 1891 to guard against this danger have not lessened the problem of the regaining of the proletarian world, which is most pressing and urgent. It is at the very core of discussions which have been had within the Church since the opening of the present century.

Another problem, likewise difficult, has more lately revealed itself. Linked to the kind of capitalism which was born of the industrial revolution, the colonial system is crumbling before our eyes. Members of races other than the white race have reclaimed and obtained the right to direct their own destinies. Without expressly desiring it, the Church sometimes benefited from the facilities which the colonial system presented to it. Despite the generosity and the disinterestedness which it has shown to colonial peoples, does not the Church now run the risk of being affected by the changing order of things? This is a prime reason why the problems involved in the attainment of independence by the Afro-Asiastic peoples claim the Church's most serious attention. There is, moreover, another reason for her involvement. These new nations are poor, their people are to be categorized as "underdeveloped." The desire to evangelize has to be united to, even yield place to, the need for charity.

After all, some simple statistics will allow us to estimate the grave nature of the situation in which the Church finds herself. The population of the world numbers approximately three billion human beings. Upward of 1,900,000,000 of them are not Christian at all, and among the Christians, according to the standards by which Catholicity is determined, between 480,000,000 and 510,000,000 can be reckoned to be Catholics. Doubtless, these figures justify the relatively optimistic assurance that the proportion of Catholics throughout the world has not changed: there were, in 1880, 212,000,000 Catholics out of 1,300,000,000 inhabitants. But do not these figures lead to an illusion? The investigations of Father Naidenoff abundantly prove that the countries where demographic pressure is strongest are those in which Christianity counts for least. In Western Europe, demographic increase has not reached 0.7%; it is 2.1% in the whole of Asia, and 2.5% in China. The Church of Christ knows, from now on, that it is a minority group in the world. Hence arises its obligation to reconsider its apostolic methods among non-Christians, and, at the same time, among those who are Christians only by convention. Thus, arises the need, more and more sharply felt, to reforge the links between all those who, under diverse obediences, claim kinship with the Gospel of Christ.

Finally, it would be absurd to attempt to ignore the fact that all these problems also present themselves on the political level. Some political systems claim to express in their institutions the rights proper to human reason, the yearning for social justice of the proletarian masses, and the thrust to liberty of peoples but lately colonized. At the same time, these systems make use of methods to attain these ends which the Church cannot, in principle, admit. Hence, the problem of totalitarianism, and especially of Marxist totalitarianism, faces the Church. Here again, as but yesterday in regard to liberalistic doctrines, a condemnation in principle, however necessary it may seem, is not enough. What is required is an effort at consideration, an essay in creativity, to offer to the world a Christian solution to the highly difficult problem of preserving liberty without sacrificing mankind, to preserve mankind without sacrificing liberty. What has been called, since the last century—and the term is, perhaps, both inexact and insufficient—"social Catholicism" was never set before the Church with greater urgency than it is to-day.

Succinct as it may be, this enumeration brings out the extraordinary seriousness as well as the tangled nature of the problems which the Church faces as our twentieth century has entered upon its latter half. In substance, it can be said that we are witnessing the birth of a civilization founded on technology, a civilization which will be "planetarised" to take a word from Teilhard de Chardin. It is a matter of discovering whether Christianity will continue to be a "ferment," the "salt of the earth" which its Master said it was to be. The perplexities, at once confused and ardent, which stirred within so many consciences, believing or not, from the moment it was announced that all those entrusted with the custody of the infallible deposit of faith would rally round the visible head of the Church, can, in the last analysis, have no other meaning. Millions of men expect that, through the council, the Church will reply to all these problems. And they expect that it will reply not alone with its intelligence but with its heart.

6. DOCTRINAL PERSPECTIVES

THEREFORE it is by giving thought to the problems which the epoch presents to the Church that one can arrive at an idea of the points to which the council may address its attention. This idea has already been brought out by a great many declarations emanating from authoritative sources, beginning with the most authoritative of all, as well as by semi-official statements on the part of bishops and theologians. The whole body of this information affords reason for the conclusion that the schedules of the council will cover four categories, or, to put it more happily, that they may be placed in four different perspectives: doctrinal, pastoral, apostolic and missionary, and ecumenical.

In regard to the doctrinal perspective it is well to make a distinction. In a televised interview, Cardinal Tardini declared: "I will freely say that this will be a council given over to actual, practical matters, rather than a council specifically doctrinal." And the Pope, in his message of November 14, 1960, to the members of the preparatory commissions let it be clearly understood that the proclamation of new dogmas would not be the principal end of the assembly. The fact remains, nonetheless, that the fathers of the council possess the right to raise doctrinal propositions, and the study of dogmatic definitions is not excluded. There are those who already speak of some official recognition of the rôle played by Our Lady in the Redemption.

But the fact that it can be said that there is little likelihood of the council proclaiming dogmas does not mean that there will not be considerable doctrinal activity during its sessions. It is evident that a council is, first of all, a theological assembly, and even when it reaches practical decisions, it founds them on a doctrinal base. Inasmuch as some of the most serious problems which the Church faces are, as has been seen, problems of doctrine, doctrinal consideration is necessary to solve them.

Some voices have already asked for a solemn condemnation of the heresies of the contemporary world, which would call down anathemas on theoretical and practical materialism, and also for an affirmation of God's transcendence and of the supernatural purpose of man and of human life. The task is more difficult than may appear at first glance, for, in our day, error does not present itself solely under some definite and clear-cut form as in the time of Arius or the age of Luther and Calvin. Canon Vancourt has justly observed that "it is rather a matter of a certain environment, a kind of intellectual climate, colored by ideas, more or less current, which runs abroad one knows not how and which affect us in spite of ourselves." It will not be easy to take action against such an imponderable. Is not a middle-class man who has his children baptized, who gives his daughter a church wedding, and looks forward to Christian burial for himself, despite the fact that, in every other department of his life, he is wholly enmeshed in the scramble for money and material comfort, is he not a greater "materialist" than the Communist workman who gives over to his cause a third of his income and lives for an ideal? At whom should the condemnation be launched?

The one thing that is certain is that condemnation, pure and simple (should it, in some sense, be necessary), would not be enough.* And, furthermore, there are cases in which it could be both ineffective and dangerous. The bishops of Holland have appropriately pointed out that we live in so pluralistic a milieu, in which Christians and non-Christians are so enmeshed and associated one with another, that any rad-

---

* Many have sought to draw from the Council a solemn warning to Western society against the erotism which tends, more and more, to fashion morals and manners in the press, the cinema, and the radio.

ical separation of them is impossible. And, again, it is impossible to turn away from the thought of the millions of Christians who lie under the heel of their enemies and who are held as hostages.

Our day has less need of hearing anathemas than of being plainly instructed in a doctrine which would make clear the Christian meaning of man and society, a doctrine stated in terms pertinent to twentieth-century man. "It is our intimate conviction," John XXIII has said, "that the Lord truly wishes to make use of the council as a means to lead souls to real and vital participation in truth." Here again, it is a question of the attitude which one should take toward contemporary life which is seen to bulk largest in the discussion of what Vatican II will mean, just as this same question dominated the period in which Vatican I met. Historical experience attests that the best attitude is not one of summary denial. So prudent a theologian as Father Spiazzi has gone so far as to say, in a conference which *Osservatore Romano* published on March 21, 1959, that one of the doctrinal tasks of the council will be to plot out the place of the Church "in face of the degenerative forms of contemporary systems of thought, especially materialism, laicism, and historicism, because it must be remembered that each enshrines a particle of truth which ought to be preserved and become integrated within the Christian synthesis." His words are worth keeping in mind, for they reveal a propensity not to anathematize but rather to engage in dialogue. A positive effort is expected of the conciliar fathers. Their way to it has been in preparation for a century, and sights have been set not only by the Popes in their great encyclicals, but by many a solitary scholar, as well. What remains to be done is to synthesize all this data. The fathers must also deal with certain propositions offered by Christian thinkers in efforts to resolve the problems of our age, as for example, those concerned with the question of science and religion; and they will have to indicate to what degree such efforts are acceptable from the Catholic viewpoint.

A further doctrinal result is looked for from the council and there is a good deal of evidence that this will be forthcoming. This effort, according to Father Spiazzi, "will have reference to the integral reality of the Church as being the mystical body of Christ, in visible and social form." This is to say, there may be expected from the assembly a theology of the Church. Such an attempt was foreshadowed as early as the time of Trent; and, during the nineteenth century, through the work of Moehler, Padre Passaglia, and Scheeben, real progress was made in developing a theology of the Church. During the time of preparation for the First Vatican Council, a schedule *De Ecclesia* was indeed drawn up; but while it was forward-looking in some directions—in regard, for example, to the Mystical body—it was quite inadequate along some other lines. We have already seen how some chapters of this schedule were detached from it and put on the priority list of matters to be voted on at the council; these were the portions which had to do with the prerogatives of the Pope. What was in view at the time was that this *Constitutio prima*, containing the proclamation of infallibility, would be followed by a *Constitutio secunda*, in which all that concerns the other parts of the Church would be taken up. In that event, however, the interruption of the council prevented any work in this direction.

Since that time a number of texts and books have been published and have notably developed this matter. The encyclical, *Mystici Corporis*, of Pius XII looms up as a lighthouse in this connection. It is impossible to enumerate here all the writing which, in diverse languages, have contributed to form Catholic thought in knowledge of the Church: the list is an immense one, ranging from works of E. Mersch to those of Tromp (the present secretary of the Preparatory Committee

on Theology), and from those of Father Congar and Father
de Lubac to those of Mura and Dabin. All these studies can
issue, in the future, in a *Summa de Ecclesia*, wherein the
Church might be defined and portrayed according to its supernatural reasons for being, as well as in its organizational methodology. If thought is given to the chief matters which have
been under study since the First Vatican Council closed, it
might appear that a theology of the Church would be principally concerned with three points. It could make clear that
Papal primacy does not necessarily bring in its train uniform-
ity, dead-leveling, wholesale centralization, and the extinction
of all authority subordinate to it; for, since the unity of the
Church is, henceforth, an accepted proposition, there can be
admitted to exist, within the bosom of that unity, a supple-
ness of organization, a lawful diversity. On the other hand, it
can bring into relief that sense of the Church as a community,
that sense which is one of the great discoveries of recent times,
in order that it be well understood by all—including the great
body of lay Christians—that all have their place, all have a role
to play. This requires that a just attempt be made to read correctly the lesson which stems from the great work of Catholic
action and the movements of the lay apostolate. And finally,
it can sketch out the attitude which the Church must present
in a world disposed to *planetary thinking*, taking note of all
the cultural expressions which can be used to support and to
serve the body of revelation, no longer restricted to identify-
ing itself with the West where Christianity, up to the present,
has so deeply sunk its roots.

Abbé Jean Frisque has wisely observed that "a theology
of apostolic action is the key to a worthwhile answer to
questions which, today, confront the Church." And Jan
Mayendorff has emphasized in his book, *L'Eglise Ortho-
doxe*, that the problem of unity is linked to ecclesiologi-
cal positions among which the council will have to make a

choice. The future of Christian lay-action is not less dependent upon this, as are, likewise, the chances of an apostolate in the Afro-Asiatic world, to say nothing of the Church's possibilities of surviving in the parts of the world which are dominated by communism. There is no doubt that the statement of a theology of the Church appropriate to the current situation will be first and foremost among the hopes of the conciliar fathers.

7. PASTORAL PERSPECTIVES

"WE EXPECT great things from this council, which will wish to effect a renewal of Faith's strength, of doctrine, and of ecclesiastical discipline, as well as of religious and spiritual life, and to contribute to the fulfillment of the Christian principles which are at once its own inspiration and the foundation of all progress in civic, economic, and social life." These words from the Pope's allocution of November 14, 1960, to the members of the preparatory committees, sufficiently show the importance which he attaches to what can be called the inner working of the council, to that self-effort which must be exercised if a renewal of the Church's life is to be brought about. And both Cardinal Tardini and Cardinal Montini have said many things which show the same kind of expectation. Of the twelve committees or secretariats which are engaged in preparing the council, at least eight are charged with concerns of this kind. Pastoral work, which, to put matters in a nutshell, is the exercise of that science, or ordered body of knowledge, which governs the relationship between the Church and the faithful, has been in the very forefront of the preoccupations of the Catholic world during the last fifteen years. There can be no doubt that it will, likewise, be given a place of priority in the council.

The end in view is evident: it is a matter of promoting a religion which will be effective, a religion which knows how to speak to our contemporaries in a way which will touch their hearts. But the means by which this end is to be attained are far from being simple to discover and easy to put into practice. For, as John XXIII has said, "on every hand, the battlelines are drawn against what is good and true," and, on every hand, there are "temptations and the lure of material advantage." Pastoral work is easy in times when men's consciences are thoroughly colored by Christian principles, even though their actions may give the lie to their Christian profession; but, today, even in great sectors of a world calling itself Christian, it is pagan custom which guides men. "We are at the point," as Msgr. Jaeger profoundly notes, "of beholding the end of the era inaugurated by Constantine, during which Christianity has been at the root of thought, serving as the lode-star of men's acts." This implies a need for new methods of approach to problems; and one knows the difficulty of attempting to change the methodology of institutions which have an age-long history . . .

Therefore the pastoral perspectives which lie before the council are perspectives of vast length, and the fields in which decision must be made are of infinite variety. They concern, first of all, the system under which pastoral work is exercised, that is to say the disposition and the use to be made of the men and the means which the Church has at hand. There are those who think that, in a world where the telephone and the automobile bulk so large, the parish organisation is no longer suited to current life, and that, if it be allowed to retain its liturgical radius, this should be determined on a vaster scale with a view to the exercise of pastoral work on a broader scale; and they point to "regional missions" as already offering examples of such a solution of the problem. There are specialists, even more bold, who think that it is at the level of whole dioceses, or ecclesiastical provinces, or even of whole nations, that pastoral problems are set, and that it is at such a level that they must be considered, in a fashion, of course, which would safeguard the Church's unity.

The study of the disposition of pastoral work necessarily leads to the consideration of the problem of the apportionment of the clergy. It scarcely seems logical that, within the same country, there should be some dioceses cruelly hampered by a lack of priests whereas others have almost an oversupply. In France, generous efforts have already been made to respond to this problem, and some dioceses "rich in priests," like Luçon in La Vendée, have sent some of them into less well-supplied dioceses. On the international scene, priests from Europe or from North America have been sent into Latin America. Many of these are Canadians. Will the council show awareness of these attempts and will it read aright the lesson they give?

A closely related question concerns the assistance which can be given by monks and religious in pastoral duties. And finally, it need not be said that one of the great and pressing concerns of the council will have to do with the training of priests, for, in the last analysis, the vitality of the Church and its influence upon the mass of men depends on their work. It has been shown, as a result of many enquiries undertaken among the laity, that the unanimous wish of the faithful is for priests who will be both highly spiritual and saintly while remaining simple and easy of approach by those who are troubled. On the other hand, enquiries among the clergy indicate that they wish to be less isolated, and to have more companionship and assistance in their spiritual concerns as well as in their actual daily lives.

If, despite all efforts at reorganization, the number of clergy should still be insufficient in certain places, can they not be given assistants? For some little time, there has been current in the Church a wish to accord to the diaconate—that oft-times disdained office—something of the importance which belongs to it. Father Epagneul, founder of the Missionary Brethren of the Countryside, and periodicals like *Evangeliser* and *Wohrt und Warbeit*, attach great importance to this notion. Deacons who do not intend to proceed to the reception of priestly orders might even be permitted to marry; they could serve as auxiliaries to the clergy in a great many of their tasks, notably in that of giving religious instruction.

But the great problem in the whole matter of the reorganization of pastoral resources concerns the role to be taken by the laity in the Church and of the function which they can fulfill in the work of spreading the Gospel. And, moreover, it is not merely in order to make up for the lack of priests that the laity are to be called on to take a major share in the church's work: it is because, as was said by Saint Avitus (a bishop in Dauphiné in the age of barbarism), and, as has been said lately by Bishop de Bazelaire: "the laity are the Church." One of the preparatory committees has been specifically deputed to study the apostolate of the laity and their place in Catholic action movements as well as in works of charity and education. Nevertheless, it is also the function of the Theological Committee to set forth a true "theology of the lay state," which will be an integrated part of the theology of the Church. Père Congar, a member of the Theological Committee, has already, in an important book, sketched out a "plan" for a theology of the lay state. Will there come into being those *seminaries—or religious-training schools—for the laity* which some have suggested should be instituted? Shall we see the council proclaiming that "royal priesthood of believers" of which Abbé Dabin speaks.

As the ordered body of principles underlying the relationship between the Church and its followers, pastoral theology must likewise be concerned with the manner in which Christ's

Gospel is spread. Hence there arise numerous problems. By and large, they may all be summed up in a few words. What is in question here is the matter of presenting the word of God to those whom it is intended to reach, and doing so in a manner which affords them the opportunity of hearing and receiving it. This poses two kinds of questions. Technology has placed at man's disposal new ways of communication: the press, the radio, television, and the moving pictures. The Church has already made use of new means: the Catholic press has become a most efficacious means through which it imparts Christian principles and Christian information to the great masses who do not attend Church services. In the United States, the apostolate through the use of television has met with outstanding success: what Bishop Fulton Sheen has done in this field is well-known. A special secretariate of the council is studying the problems raised by all the new means for the diffusion of ideas, and this will be most useful.

But is it enough to be ready to employ the radio (or the cinema,) the press and television? It is more than ever necessary that these new means of reaching souls be in the hands of men who know how to speak to the soul. And it cannot in any way be invariably guaranteed that such will always be the case. Among problems of the pastoral field, it seems that not enough has been said of sermons and instructions. A rather superficial enquiry of those who go to Sunday Mass and of fathers of families indicates that these seem to be of minor importance at parish Masses.

And, finally, there is an aspect of pastoral work to which much attention will undoubtedly be given by the council, for a special committee has been set up to deal with it: this is what has, for some time, been called the liturgical aspect of pastoral work. The Church is persuaded that the liturgy is not only a mystic ceremonial: it is also a way in which the believer may share in the life of the Church. Formerly, the liturgy was as

an unknown or mysterious tongue to the majority of
Catholics; most admirable efforts have been used to change this
situation. Uncounted publications and many congresses have
worked to this end. Many attempts have been made; and they
include the celebration of Mass facing the people, the dialogue
Mass in which the congregation reads certain of the Mass formularies aloud with, or in response to, the celebrating priest,
the reading of certain parts of the liturgical texts in the ver-
nacular. Some of these have given occasion for spirited discussion, and Claudel has said: "This is the Mass with the wrong
side foremost." Some principles must be established; some
general regulation seems necessary; and it cannot be doubted
that this will be one of the tasks of the coming council.

8. MISSIONARY AND APOSTOLIC PERSPECTIVES

Although the council, as an assembly of the Church,
must, first of all, devote itself to the internal problems of the
Church, it is also true that it cannot afford to ignore other
questions which, even though they concern non-Christian
elements, touch upon the essential meaning of the Church, and
the very meaning of the Christian Gospel. The great words of
Jesus to His disciples: "Go and teach all nations" have established forever one of the major characteristics of Christianity:
the necessity of spreading it. It is not a mere matter of prop-
agandizing, as is the case with a political party, instead, it vests
in a Christian an obligation to be an apostle, because he knows
that he must render an account to God in respect to the spread
of truth, and because he feels himself burdened by the immense
number of souls who, all over the globe, are seeking for
enlightenment. Apostolic and missionary perspectives, in-
timately linked with doctrinal and pastoral perspectives,

stretch, as is evident, before the council. And with them are associated ecumenical perspectives.

In the broadest possible sense of the term, the mere fact that a council is meeting is a thing of great apostolic significance. By bearing witness to its unity, to its moral nature, to its desire to be in the service of truth, the Church affirms its own nature before the whole world, Christian and non-Christian alike. It is already possible to take account of this from the sympathetic attention which has, even now, been given to the mere announcement of the council. It may be that the council will further increase the apostolic stir it has so far created by taking a stand upon the great questions which perplex twentieth century mankind. In a great many writings and statements—of a private nature, of course—which have been probing for two years the reason behind the convocation of the council, the wish is often expressed that the Church will raise its voice and launch a loud cry of warning against the great dangers which nuclear might can visit upon humankind. Another perplexing problem can also come before the council; it is that of famine among men. And, related to this, is the matter of help for under-developed peoples. Already, as is well-known, organisms like Catholic Charities have worked to make effective the charity of Christ. Some think that by occupying itself with matters on the moral level, and by recalling to nations having more than they need the undeniable Gospel obligation to share their abundance with those who do not have enough, the council will have already accomplished an apostolic work of definite import.

The will to exercise the apostolate has shown itself concretely, these many centuries, by the fact that the Church has established organisms which have striven to implant Christianity wherever it is unknown: these are the missions. Formerly, the word was used only of attempts to evangelize the heathen, such as were undertaken by Saint Francis Xavier

in the Indies or by Saint Isaac Jogues and Saint Jean de Bre-
beuf among American Indians. In the seventeenth century, another sense became current, and with Michel de Nobletz, Saint
John Eudes, Saint Vincent de Paul, and Saint Grignion de
Montfort, the word was employed in a pastoral sense to convey efforts made at the revivification of faith among Christians themselves. Our own time has seen a third sense come
into use with the discovery, by sociologists, that there are
whole sectors, sometimes very large ones, within zones theoretically Christian, where paganism is totally dominant. The
noted book by Abbé Godin and Abbé Daniel, *France, pays des
mission?* has accustomed men to this sense of the word.

Today, there is every evidence that the work of the apostolate ought be exercised among two great classes of mankind
—those who do not know Christianity and those who have
forgotten it. In the interests of the latter, much preparatory
work has already been undertaken, especially during the past
fifteen years, which have witnessed a double effort. On the one
side, due to progress made in Christian sociology, especially
under the impulsion provided by Gabriel Le Bras, the Church
has gained extensive knowledge of this problem and has discovered that the proletarian city dwellers of the West, and
even some among the rural areas, are as far from the faith as
ever were the Kafirs or the Samoyedic peoples before the
coming of the missionaries. And did not the Roman Synod
of Autumn, 1960, reveal that the very suburbs of the Eternal
City constitute a *mission land?* On the other hand, the situation
having been seen to be what it is, attempts have been made
to remedy it. For example, as Bishop Veuillot writes:

> There is no one who will not think of what has been called
> the experiment of the *Worker Priests*. This was—and remains
> —the symbol of a generous effort, if sometimes a rash one, of
> these apostles of the Church to penetrate the world of the
> workers. The Holy See wishes this attempt at apostolic penetra-

tion to be continued, but under new conditions and with surer safeguards. It may fall to the lot of the council to state fundamental norms more precisely.*

It appears that this effort to set in place a duly qualified missionary effort is not to be confined solely to certain sectors thought of in terms of social definition. It is a tragic discovery of recent years that countries long Christian, namely those of Latin America, are in danger of seeing the Church come apart at the seams, that they are already poisoned by a paganization underwritten by Marxist propaganda. Under these conditions pastoral work and missionary work overlap, and it is only by the actual pooling of means, already initiated, as has been seen, that results can be hoped for. If one may take account of the many official and non-official statements which have confessed concern on this score, it will have to be admitted that the problem of Latin America will be among those which the council must solve.

What was formerly called the "missionary question" henceforth presents itself to the Church under a new form. The end of the colonial system and the "coming of political age" of non-white peoples re-opens fundamental matters. Less and less will the new Afro-Asiatic nations tolerate a Christianity which presents itself as linked not only to the colonial regime but even to white culture and the Western manner of thought. It was not only for his own time that Saint Paul, the master missionary, said that in order to gain souls for Christ he would have to make of himself "a Greek among the Greeks." Down through the centuries, the Church has numbered in its ranks men who have prophetically recalled to it this ancient obligation: such were Father Matteo Ricci and Father de Nobili. Today, the Church knows that the ful-

---

* In a courageous article in *Masses ouvrières* of April, 1961, Abbé Michonneau recalls to us that the true problem is "the hiatus which intervenes between the working class and the Church."

fillment of this obligation is essential to its own nature. Before
the triple assault of indigenous nationalism, Islam, and communism, it cannot hope to retain its chances except by enter-
ing into the full current of history, which means by being
faithful to its characteristic vocation.

The real problems which lie before the council, in this missionary perspective, are therefore not primarily concerned
with the difficulties caused by the insufficiency, and insufficiency absurd and almost ridiculous, in the number of the
"missionaries" when set alongside the task they must perform.
It will rather be a question of showing on the ideological
plane, within the framework of that "theology of the church"
which has already been spoken of, that, as was admirably said
by John XXIII when he spoke to the Second World Congress
of Colored Writers and Artists, "The Church does not identify
itself with any one culture, not even with Western culture
despite the fact that its history is closely bound up with it,"
that, in the discharge of its apostolic mission, it will be faithful to the law of the Incarnation, that it does not seek to trans-
plant directly among the younger nations the structure of old
forms of Christianity, and that it admits and wishes for a black
Christian culture, a yellow Christian culture, each having its
own characteristic intellectual methodology, its own modes of
expression, its own kind of art,—that, in a word, it would no
longer occur to anyone to construct, as was done in the past,
a Gothic cathedral at Peking.

On the practical level, the council will find a path traced
out for it by the Popes of this century who took the initiative
in encouraging the development of indigenous Christianities
by giving them their own episcopates: Pius XI consecrated
the first bishops of the yellow race; Pius XII named the first
bishops of the black race, and later raised Far Eastern prelates
to the rank of cardinal; John XXIII created the first Negro
cardinal. The importance which the council will accord to

the new churches of the non-white races is abundantly established by the place given their representatives in the assembly. As has been noted above, this place is four times what it would be had a strictly proportional calculation been made. And there can be no doubt that there will have to be studied some particular problems which concern the non-white churches, such as the very delicate matter of the limitation of births, which certain Asian Christianities cannot ignore. Doubtless, the Pope had in mind the immense tasks before the council, as well as all the world expects from it, by way of result, when he asked that all pray for energy and strength in the search for whatever will best correspond to current needs in apostolic work.

9. ECUMENICAL PERSPECTIVES

FINALLY, there lie before the council ecumenical perspectives, beyond the pressing current needs of the apostolate, beyond doctrinal preoccupation, although including these and, as a matter of fact, being the sources of their real significance. It will be recalled that it was the Pope himself who pointed to these perspectives on the very day he first made known his plan to convoke the council. Moreover, it is beyond question that, even prior to his election to Peter's Chair, he had pondered on the great problem posed by the disunity of Christians. His secretary, Bishop Capovilla has revealed, in a moving conference published by *Osservatore Romano* on December 31, 1959, that in preparing some remarks to be made in 1953 at his installation as Patriarch of Venice, the then Bishop Roncalli had written that "having had to do with people of varying religious and philosophical ideas" he had always been "more concerned—with, of course, due deferral to the fundamentals of Catholic belief and morality—with that which is shared than which separates . . ." It is just such a view which has animated the decision of John XXIII to bring together a council. Far from being an instrument of political calculation, this project of his is a manifestation of the outpourings of a heart in which the charity of Christ is brilliantly alive.

From the very beginning, the appeal for unity has touched the heart-strings of the public, as Father Wenger observed, and it has thus aroused their immediate interest. For reasons already referred to, the press has laid great stress on this aspect of the project at the very time that it has neglected others. Readily might readers of the newspapers be convinced that the one aim of the council is to achieve what has long been called "the union of the churches." The impression was so strong, and the risk of erroneous opinion being formed so great, that the Pope himself restated the whole matter by declaring precisely, in several addresses as early as April, 1959, and then later in the Encyclical, *Ad Petri Cathedram* of June 29, 1959, that the chief end of the council would be "to further the development of the Catholic faith, the moral renewal of Christian discipline to the needs and methods of our time." He then concluded with the observation that the sight of this being undertaken would of itself constitute "a gentle summons to separated Christians to seek unity." Has this more precise statement been misunderstood? As far as Catholics are concerned, it could only be so by those who are unaware of what Canon Law stipulates of an ecumenical council, and who are lacking in sufficient knowledge of the ample tasks that lie before the Church. Misunderstanding is more easily to be accounted for as far as non-Catholics are concerned, and observers at the Munich *Kirchentag* caught echoes of this as early as the Autumn of 1959. Yet it was necessary that the papal statement be made; for it would have been most dangerous to permit the growth in the mind of the public any notion that the council will be a kind of interconfessional congress where the churches, sects, and denominations of every kind will be represented in the hope that, out of the confusion of debate, there might miraculously emerge a union of all the baptized.

To speak in concrete terms, the importance which the Church accords to the problem of unity can be expressed by noting that, of twelve organisms which are charged with making preparations for the council, one alone is consecrated to unity. This is the Special Secretariate for the Union of Christians, whose mission has been defined by the Pope himself in these terms: "It must make evident our love and our good will to those who, bearing the name of Christians, are yet separated from the Apostolic See, so that they may be able to follow the work of the council and thus more easily find the way to rejoin that unity for which Our Lord Jesus Christ so ardently prayed to His heavenly Father." This secretariat, then, has a double purpose: it will make known to non-Catholic Christians what the council is doing, and it will serve as a channel for the reception of communications from the separated brethren. Thus will it be, in the words of its chairman, "a means to help non-Catholics achieve union." The choice of the two men who have been placed in charge of this secretariat is itself significant: both come from countries in which non-Catholics are in a majority, and both are thoroughly conversant with the kind of questions which arise between Catholics and non-Catholics. They are Cardinal Bea, a German, who is a biblical specialist, and Bishop Willebrands, a Hollander, who serves also as secretary to the International Catholic Conference, a group of theologians concerned with ecumenical matters.

How can expression be given to the kind of work which the council will undertake in order to promote unity? On the one hand, by the fact that it is to function as a means of renewing Christian life and adapting the Church to the needs of our time, it will do away with a number of the obstacles which nowadays act as barriers before separated brothers of good will. For example, it is undeniable that the evil conduct of Catholics militates against understanding between them and non-Catholics. By recalling Catholics to their Christian duty, the council will be furthering union. Another example— should the traditionally accepted organizational forms of the Catholic church be disturbing to certain separated brethren, a reconstitution of them may be enough to remove the difficulty. This is as much as to say that the whole function of the council, whether doctrinal—notably so in what concerns the theology of the Church—pastoral, apostolic or missionary, will contribute to preparing the paths of unity. Father Congar has picturesquely summed it up by saying, "The council will be wholly attuned to unity."

And, on the other hand, by its definitive work, the council can help separated brothers find the path to union. Now and henceforth, this is the very task of the Secretariate for Unity. Cardinal Bea has clearly set forth in the course of many interviews, conferences, and articles, just what the secretariat will be concerned with. It will do its work in a spirit of wholehearted objectivity, "by noting whatever is held in common by diverse non-Catholic bodies and the Roman Catholic Church in regard to doctrine, worship, and organization, and by determining what differences exist. Then it will ascertain the desires of the separated brothers for the attainment of union; and, finally, it will determine the course of action which may best remove difficulties in the way of achieving this union."

This logging of the conditions of a common meeting ground is, as a matter of fact, something which cannot be dispensed with. History testifies well enough to the enormous importance of non-theological factors in the effort to attain unity. At the council of Florence, the theologians were in agreement, but differences in outlook, personal feelings, matters of protocol, accepted custom, even trifling prejudices gave check to success. A careful study of the conditions of union would, of itself, be enough to prevent a similar failure. Such work can be—indeed, it should be—done slowly. And, for this reason, it is important to emphasize that the Secretariat for Unity is not a mere *ad hoc* committee; it will continue to function even after the council has terminated, perhaps in the form of a Roman congregation.

All this, undeniably, reveals what spirit is abroad. It is certain that the whole problem of unity will be approached from the very beginning of Vatican II in a climate wholly new. This is not to say that, for centuries, many Catholics have not been torn with searing anguish before the scandal of disunity. One need not go further back than the last century to enumerate a dozen important attempts undertaken by Catholics to foster union. As we have seen, Pius IX wished that the Orthodox Church of the East might be represented at the First Council of the Vatican, and he even addressed a message to various Protestant bodies. Nevertheless, it is undeniable that in the hundred years that have since gone by, a great gap has been bridged. This is true not of Catholics only, but of their separated brothers as well. Although the Catholic Church did not judge it proper to participate in the meetings of the World Council of Churches, where representations of Protestantism and of Eastern Orthodoxy came together, and where, as a matter of fact, there have sometimes been Catholics present as observers, nevertheless innumerable contacts have taken place, and they have increased of late. The sensational conversations of Malines of a half-century ago have not led to the hoped-for result of a rapprochement with the Anglicans; but many are the less spectacular interchanges which since then have worked to prepare the way. For example, at the

Protestant Priory of Taizé, in Burgundy, at the end of September, 1960, a number of Protestant clergymen met with some priests, of whom six were bishops, for a series of studies and conferences. This is an example, among others, of the new attitude. Various theologians in various camps have made clear, in uncounted articles in review, "what unites and what separates." And the most striking of all signs of the newer climate is that "Octave of Prayer for Unity," which came to be in 1898 at the initiative of Paul Wattson, an Anglican priest in Maryland, who later became a convert to Catholicism. This has been spread all over the world since 1935 as a result of the efforts of Father Paul Couturier—that saintly man of our own day—and, presently, there are associated with it uncounted numbers of the devout of all obediences.

Since the announcement of the council, many acts and words demonstrate that it is not self-deception to believe that a new climate has come about. The most manifest of these, in the eyes of the larger public, was the noteworthy visit made to the Pope by the Anglican Archbishop of Canterbury, the Most Reverend Geoffrey Francis Fisher. But there can also be cited many statements which, of themselves, have great value as indicating the spirit of this new climate. Karl Barth, the outstanding theologian of Protestantism, has said: "There is a new possibility of fraternal discussion with the Church of Rome." The chief Presbyterian dignitary of the United States, Dr. Blake, declared: "The Pope has certainly contributed toward the creation of an atmosphere of union which now reigns among the Christian churches." And the Ecumenical Council of Churches issued this statement: "It is matter for rejoicing that it is now possible to hold a dialogue with the Church of Rome." Patriarch Athenagoras of Constantinople went even further by applying to John XXIII the Gospel phrase: "There was a man sent from God, and his name is John." It would not do to exaggerate the scope of these statements, but they do at least show that the chances of a meeting of minds are not merely utopian.

From the Catholic viewpoint, ecumenical perspectives can be thought of as constituting a triple imperative. The first is an imperative which impels toward sincerity. What is in question is not a matter of historical investigation; there should be no attempt made to determine, yet once more, who was at fault and who was in the right. What must be faced as the starting point is the doleful fact of disunion, the common disobedience of all Christians to the order of the Master: "that all be one." And there must be a sincere resolution to put an end to this.

There is an imperative of charity. With admirable force, Cardinal Bea has written:

> Too often has Catholic intransigency in dogmatic matters—and dogma is something absolutely necessary—embodied the memory of past battles and old wounds and has served only to contract and harden the hearts of all: it may lead, though not always, to hatred. But it certainly may engender indifference and an attitude of irresponsibility. We must, not in words alone, but in deed, as well, consider our separated brothers, as real brothers, as Saint Augustine has so wondrously put it, in words which the Holy Father recalls to us in his Encyclical, *Ad Petri Cathedram*, 'Whether or not they will it so, they are our brothers. They shall not cease to be our brothers until they cease to say: *Our Father* . . .'

There is, moreover, an imperative to fidelity. As John XXIII has put it: "Fidelity to the Church, one, holy, catholic, apostolic, and Roman . . . for Jesus Christ did not institute many Churches . . . but only one, the Apostolic and Universal Church. This is the Church of Rome, the true Mother of all peoples, splendid in the variety of its rites, but ever one in faith, discipline, order, and sacred functioning."

Even were it to make it easier for the separated brothers to come to it, there are matters about which the Church cannot compromise. These concern her doctrines, first of all, but there are also matters which bear upon her divine foundation. This is a position which permits of no essential deviation; it is definitive, and to a Catholic the expression of his whole-hearted fidelity to the truth he has received from God; it is of all exactions the most exacting, involving his obedience to the unity which God Himself has willed to be; it is a stand which can never be renounced.

It is by its obedience to the compulsion of this three-fold imperative that the council—by which I mean, in the present circumstance, the secretariate which is preparing the council's agenda—that the council must plot out a way. There is no point in hiding from ourselves or others the fact that it will be a difficult course to plot, that it is choked with many difficult obstacles. Many a time have the most authoritative voices proclaimed that we must not "expect a miracle." Father Florovsky, the Orthodox theologian, believes that a long time of preparation will be needed before any concrete results can be had, and that, at the moment, neither East nor West is spiritually ready to attain unity quickly. Vatican II will not be "the Council of Union." One cannot, within the space of a few months, put an end to a centuries old separation—nine hundred years apart as far as the Orthodox are concerned; four hundred years the Protestants. But the council will prepare the way. And already there will have been wrought a great work if, in every camp, the preparation proceed in good will, in sincere resolution to accomplish the will of Christ in shared enthusiasm of all hearts.

10. THE COUNCIL OF JOHN XXIII

SUCH ARE the larger perspectives into which one may logically orient the opening of the council. Is this to suggest that it is only such problems as so summary a view has brought to light will be the sole subjects of consideration? To believe that would be both presumptuous and absurd. An ecumenical council is not to be compared to one of those meetings in which the share-holders of large industrial or commercial corporations come together periodically to ratify the decisions of a board of directors who have themselves made up the agenda in order that resolutions which they alone have prepared may be voted upon. Although the council is dependent upon the Pope, having been convoked by him, organized by him, and although it will await the confirmation by him of the decisions it will make, it should not be believed that it has no autonomy of character. The conciliar fathers, it must be remembered, have the right to bring forward their own proposals, and *a priori*, there is no reason to assume that they will not exercise this right. In so large a gathering of men, currents can be produced which will force into priority matters which have not previously been considered as being of first importance. What must not be overlooked is this: the council meets under the shadow of the Holy Spirit; it is theologically sound to observe that the Third Person of the Blessed Trinity is at work, and that he will effectively guide all the men—every one of them consecrated by Him—who sit in the council. There is no more likelihood that an attempt will be made to set limits to the Spirit's scope and the constant opportunities of enlightenment which He gives to those who entrust themselves to His guidance, than there is that the council will tempt the Holy Spirit, or resist Him, as has sometimes been said.

There will assuredly reign at Vatican II a liberty of spirit which can be fruitful in provoking initiative. The retired Archbishop of Bombay, Bishop Roberts, whom I have already quoted on several occasions, has had something pertinent to say of this liberty; and to his remarks Bishop Veuillot adds his own guarantee. "In a universal council," says Bishop Roberts, "the bishops are independent of all manner of influences, and this is not merely because they are freed by the Holy Spirit, but also because they find themselves face to face with other bishops influenced in widely different ways." If there are some nations today which have not scrupled to limit the physical liberty of their bishops, may there not exist, in other nations, other forms of subjection which may tend to limit the bishops in the fuller exercise of their freedom?

"A general council helps these bishops," as the same prelate goes on to say, "to put into subordination to their true dignity, which is that of successors of Christ's Apostles, every other loyalty which they may own. Assembled in ecumenical convocation, at the call of the Supreme Pontiff, Catholic bishops more easily escape from the circumstances and limitations which may customarily restrict their vision and their activity; outshining the differences of race and tongue, they can reveal in truth and simplicity their high ecclesiastical function at the very time that they offer to the world a manifest indication of the unity of the Church and its universal character."

This liberty of the spirit will be able to exert itself at Vatican II all the more so because the confrontation of men and of ideas will take place on so vast a scale. Never before in its history has the Church seen an assembly of some 2,500 bishops. Never before has it seen Anglo-Saxon Catholicism, hitherto barely tolerated, now strong in its eighty million adherents, bring to a council its youthful dynamism. Never has it seen under the snowy mitres worn at solemn session, dozens, even hundreds, of black- or yellow-skinned faces. Herein will the ecumenicity of the Church be affirmed in a striking spectacle which the cinema and the television will open to the whole world. No one is able to say, in advance of the event, what things, great and new, may emerge from this gigantic mingling of so many men and ideas, of so much solicitude and experience. But one can measure the genius of that inspired man who, by launching the Church upon this great adventure, has by the same token, suggested to it perils and eventualities which can scarcely be imagined.

In every way, and in every sense, Vatican II will be the Council of John XXIII. It is he who has willed to convoke it, he alone, standing before God's face. He it is who has given to it its ends, of which the culmination will be to prepare the way for union with separated brothers. He it is who, at once, established the rhythmic pace of the council, a work meticulously planned but one to be consummated in a great surge of fervency. He it is who has wished, even in the choice he has made of the men appointed to arrange the conciliar preparations, to indicate his concern that discussion be wholly free, to an extent which the Church's adversaries do not even dream of. If it be true that the atmosphere in which a council meets be almost on a par with its agenda, then one can formulate a clear and definite picture of the climate in which Vatican II will convene.

This climate can be described by two words: it will be a climate colored by *truth*, a climate colored by *generosity*. The council will approach the problems which confront it honestly, clear-headedly, intelligently, not abandoning itself to will-o-the-wisp illusions, but having the intent really to look into the difficulties which face the Church, the grave perils which menace it, so that solutions may be reached which will match the facts of life. But it will also concern itself with men, in a spirit of true and entire charity, by showing that it knows how to make the relevant distinction, in respect to adversaries, between the doctrine which must be reprobated and the men who are to be respected and loved, by emphasizing what unites hearts and consciences while freeing the Church of all that might serve to obscure its welcoming brilliance. Already there have been offered to our separated brothers many signs of affection. In expressing the intentions of the Week of Prayer for Unity, the Pope has replaced words like *return* and *submission* with the term *reconciliation*. And, at the same time, he suppressed, in liturgical formularies, certain expressions which Moslems and Jews had found offensive, just as he is now giving consideration to setting up a subcommittee to study the relations between the Church and Israel. This is indeed, it would seem, what has been hoped for by mankind throughout the world as they have greeted the announcement of the council with so much good will. Even those who are farthest from the Church know dimly all that Christ means: they expect that the council will reveal Him to them in a way that they can understand and reach, so that they may come to that Christ whose arms are ever open, who speaks to each man and calls him by name.

And it is in this wise, also, that Vatican II will truly be the council of John XXIII. A man gifted with insight, whose keen discernment of what is merely peripheral mitigates its sharpness by a watchful and smiling irony; a man of realistic leaning, more disposed to the making of practical decisions than given to abstract speculation, but whose sense of the compulsions of evident necessity goes hand in hand with his reliance upon the strength which is given from on high; a man constant in his realization that God is God, in whom the certain knowledge that he is His witness and His instrument is balanced by a sense of his own unworthiness so real that ceremonial veneration disturbs him and makes even the title of Holy Father—as he himself has said—somewhat disturbing to him, John XXIII would seem to have been providentially given to us at this point in the world's history to typify the Christ whom mankind awaits. This child of the people, now become the outstanding man of his time, the Vicar of Christ; this peasant, whose own brothers are, even now, tilling the land in Bergamo, is called by Providence to set before the face of toiling men, who endure and who hope, the very aspect of the Church which can most movingly speak to their hearts.* On the eve of the council, as pilgrims have seen him in the Vatican Library, as crowds have gazed upon him in the streets of Rome and even in its prisons, Angelo Roncalli comes forth, with hands stretched out, and with a smile on his face says: "Come, my brothers, and see that this is the Church of Christ."

* How meaningful is the fact that, by an Apostolic Letter under date of March 16, 1961, the Pope has named as patron of the council Saint Joseph —Joseph, the carpenter of Nazareth.

TRANSLATOR'S NOTE

It is with a very special sense of gratitude that I acknowledge valuable assistance, generously given me in the preparation of this translation, by my colleague at Hunter College, Dr. Rose-Marie Daele, *Officier dans l'Ordre des Palmes Académiques*.

I am also most grateful to my friends, the Rev. Professor Florence D. Cohalan, M.A., of Cathedral College, New York, and the Rev. Professor Austin Vaughn, S.T.D., of the theological faculty of St. Joseph's Seminary, Dunwoodie, New York, whose counsel on a number of special points has enabled me to solve some difficulties.

And I should like, as well, to say a word of thanks to the publishers of this English translation of M. Daniel-Rops' work, Hawthorn Books of New York, who have been most patient amid delays due to the fact that my English version of *Vatican II: Le Concile de Jean XXIII* has been prepared in the midst of academic preoccupations.

ALASTAIR GUINAN

Hunter College of the City University of New York
Feast of the Immaculate Conception of Our Lady

THE AUTHOR AND HIS BOOK

HENRI DANIEL-ROPS *is the* nom de plume *of Henri Jules Charles Petiot, born January 19, 1901, in France. The grandson of peasants and the son of an artillery officer, the young student majored simultaneously in law, geography and history, winning the equivalent of a Master's degree in each subject before he was 21 years old. Within a year he was teaching history as an associate professor, which he continued until 1945 when he retired as Professor of History at Neuilly. His nom de plume was adopted for his first book, a volume of essays published in 1926. He has used it since for his more than seventy books which include novels, historical studies, poetry, and children's books. His writings have brought him many honors, including election to the Academie Française in 1955, its youngest member. Other honors include Commander of the Order of Saint Gregory the Great, conferred by Pope Pius XII; the Grand Cross, conferred by Pope John XXIII; Grand Officer of the Order of Christ; and Officer of the Legion of Honor. He is also winner of the Academie Française' Grand Prix. His greatest successes in this country have been* This is the Mass, *and,* Jesus and His Times. *Currently he is acting as editor-in-chief of* The Twentieth Century Encyclopedia of Catholicism, *and has contributed one volume to the series as well as supervising the entire 150-volume work. He is a regular contributor to many French magazines and newspapers and edits a popular monthly magazine,* Ecclesia, *as well as publishing an intellectual quarterly. His published works in English are:* Misted Mirror (*Knopf, 1931*), Two Men in Me (*Rockwell, 1931*), The Poor and Ourselves (*Burns Oates &*

Washburn, 1938), Flaming Sword (*Cassell, 1941*), Death, Where is Thy Victory? (*Cassell, 1946*), Sacred History (*Longmans, Green, 1949*), Where Angels Pass (*Cassell, 1950*), St. Paul: Apostle of Nations (*Fides, 1953*), Jesus and His Times (*Dutton, 1954*), Book of Books (*Kenedy, 1956*), Cathedral and Crusade (*Dutton, 1957*), This is the Mass (*Hawthorn, 1958*), What is the Bible? (*part of* The Twentieth Century Encyclopedia of Catholicism: *Hawthorn, 1958*), The Heroes of God (*Hawthorn, 1959*), The Book of Mary (*Hawthorn, 1960*), Golden Legend of Young Saints (*Kenedy, 1960*), *and* Monsieur Vincent (*Hawthorn, 1961*).

THE SECOND VATICAN COUNCIL: THE STORY BEHIND THE ECU-MENICAL COUNCIL OF POPE JOHN XXIII. (*Hawthorn Books, 1962*) *was completely manufactured by the Colonial Press Inc., Clinton, Mass. The body type is Janson, designed by Anton Janson.*

A HAWTHORN BOOK